Drama Games & Improvs

Games for the classroom and beyond

Compiled, Created and Invented by
Justine Jones and Mary Ann Kelley

MERIWETHER PUBLISHING LTD.
Colorado Springs, Colorado

Meriwether Publishing Ltd., Publisher
PO Box 7710
Colorado Springs, CO 80933-7710

www.meriwether.com

Editor: Art Zapel
Assistant Editor: Audrey Scheck
Interior Design: Jan Melvin

© Copyright MMVII Meriwether Publishing Ltd.
Printed in the United States of America
First Edition

Library of Congress Cataloging-in-Publication Data

Jones, Justine, 1949-
  Drama games and improvs : games for the classroom and beyond / by Justine Jones
and Mary Ann Kelley.
     p. cm.
  Includes index.
  ISBN 978-1-56608-147-4 (pbk.)
 1. Improvisation (Acting) 2. Acting. 3. Games. I. Kelley, Mary Ann, 1948- II. Title.
  PN2071.I5J67 2007
  792.02'8--dc22
                      2007020109

        2   3   4   09   10   11

Dedication

To Sharon Smith and Cheryl Smith-Ecke, both inspirational teachers and friends, and, as always, to my son Nick and my husband Darryl.
— Justine Jones

To Charles, Chris, and Holly — my most loyal supporters, and to Justine who knows kids and knows theatre and knows how to make me work.
— Mary Ann Kelley

And to all those students who, throughout the years, played through these games and learned without knowing it, our thanks continues to go to you.
— Justine and Mary Ann

Table of Contents

Preface: How This Book Came to Be

A note from Justine Jones

When I was a junior in college, I was fortunate to receive a grant to study drama in England. I had been a theatre major at Macalester College in St. Paul, Minnesota, and was tentatively preparing for an acting career! Going to the UK changed all that. I fell into the exciting work of Drama in Education.

My first stop was in Birmingham where I studied with Peter Slade, author of *Child Drama*. Slade was arguably the first person to recognize the dynamic relationship between drama and psychology. His observations of children at play fascinated me. While at Slade's studio I met many educators, actors, and therapists from around the world, all eager to see what the connections between the two fields might be.

I was then steered back to London to meet Brian Way and experience his "developmental drama." Then it was to Newcastle to observe Dorothy Heathcote and Gavin Bolton and their amazing work in educational theatre. My head was spinning.

Back in London, I met a group of Canadians studying with Richard Courtney, author of *Play, Drama, and Thought*. They recommended that I observe Keith Johnstone's *Theatre Machine* performing in a Hampstead pub. I went and was hooked. Kindly, Keith invited me to observe his classes at the Royal Academy of Dramatic Art, and I officially became an improv groupie. Classes three times a week and performances at the pub twice weekly made up the rest of my five-month stay.

Knowing that I wanted more, I arranged with my college to spend my senior year with Richard Courtney in Victoria, British Columbia, where he had established a thriving program in Developmental Drama. Students from all over Canada and the United States flocked to the island to take his classes and study the new field of drama therapy. As a college senior, I was unclear where I fit in, but, upon graduation, I landed a job teaching high school theatre at a private school with no money for productions. My classes in improv became the theatre program, and hence the ideas of a curriculum taught primarily through improv games began.

The next year I moved to California to seek a Master's degree in Confluent Education, a new field of humanistic psychology incorporating ideas from the human potential movement in the classroom. We learned how to integrate gestalt theory and visualization techniques into the regular curriculum.

Naturally, these innovative ideas met with a great deal of opposition from more traditional educators. It became clear to me that "Theatre Arts" and "Drama" classes were much better venues for those more alternative techniques than math class.

When I landed a job teaching a full theatre arts curriculum in Aptos, California, I soon learned that expectations included much more than a simple process curriculum. I was expected to direct the fall play and the spring musical, and I needed to stage the student one-act plays. In addition, I was responsible for the forensics program and several English classes. I discovered the real work of the theatre arts classroom teacher, and it was challenging to say the least. Hence, this book.

All the theory and practice in the world does not come close to addressing the reality faced by the classroom teacher. First is the question of drama versus theatre. Drama is a process while theatre is a product. The dramatic process does not necessarily need to result in a product (performance), but that is usually the expectation. Both parents and students want to see the students perform, not just hear about what fun they had improvising. Unfortunate as we educators may find this, it is the reality of arts education in the U.S. today.

Just when I was despairing of ever being able to truly teach theatre skills through improvisation, along came Keith Johnstone's *Theatre Sportz* and then *Whose Line Is It, Anyway?* popped up on TV. Overnight, improv as performance became acceptable and, more importantly, visible. Holding a public performance of classroom drama games was something valued, not scorned. Using improvisation as part of the school talent show or to demonstrate quick creative thinking skills at open house nights was a "new" innovation. Things were looking up.

Now that drama games and improvisation are much more mainstream, developing a real curriculum using these techniques is the next step. I have been teaching on the secondary level for thirty-four years, and I can say without a doubt that improv is by far the most effective and lasting technique to use to teach acting, directing, writing, and speaking skills. The students immediately get involved and stay interested. They become performers almost immediately, introverts and extroverts alike.

This book is yours to use as you wish. The curriculum is there, but so are the games. Use what you like. Have fun! And if you wish to contact us with your own great ideas, please write us at justinewjones@gmail.com or maryann@improvideas.com.

About This Book

And Now, Some Answers

A grateful tip of the hat to the question and answer format that allows Justine and Mary Ann to answer the questions we thought you'd never ask.

Say, haven't I seen these answers before?

If you were lucky enough to purchase *Improv Ideas: A Book of Games and Lists* (also from Meriwether Publishing), you've seen something like it. Keep reading — there are answers that you haven't seen, just for this book.

I know I've seen the games before. What gives?

You're right, you've seen *some* of them. Of the 137 games in this book, fifty-five (those needing lists) appeared in *Improv Ideas: A Book of Games and Lists*. The directions are the same, but the emphasis is for the classroom. If you already have *Improv Ideas*, you won't have to work so hard on the lists. If you don't, maybe you should get a copy. There are sixteen games that don't appear in this book and tons of helpful lists made for improv.

I'm not a teacher; did I just buy the wrong book?

Are you kidding? You're the "and beyond" part of the book. Just look at the generous number of games in the book: 137 drama games! What a deal! Just bypass the lesson plans. The examples in the games work for everybody, and directors and game leaders can scan the focus questions for ideas about side coaching.

Did you make up all the games?

Many of the games are Justine's original ideas. Others are classics we learned in college or workshops with no origin given. Still others have come to us from sources long forgotten — the "Improv Grapevine," if you will. Some we adapted to our needs to such an extent that they defy provenance. Our students have also contributed games to the oeuvre from their own sources, from summer camp to drama classes in other places or times. Our own children, Nick and Chris, have also made contributions.

If we have adopted a proprietary game and are now passing it on without proper credit, please forgive us. It is not intentional.

You're kidding about a whole semester of games and improvs ... right?

Why *not* a semester of drama games? Why not a year?! Go for it. Your students will have a great time as they learn theatre through drama games and improvisation. It can all be there: characterization, plot structure, ensemble acting, creativity, the art of listening and silence, and following directions. It's sneaky because it's a way to teach drama while students think they're playing. It's adaptable enough to serve beginners or experts. It works for all age groups. Most evaluation is done on the spot and the class rarely requires homework — a bonus for people with busy schedules such as students with heavy class loads and teachers who also coach and direct.

By following this guide, teaching drama through games and improvs is amazingly disciplined while allowing for the day-to-day flexibility so often required in today's schools. Teachers can have the confidence that activities are designed to build upon the ones that precede them, yet know that the whole semester won't be ruined if a few (or even a lot) of students don't understand the point of each game or miss class due to illness or other activities. As most of the lessons are only a day long and repetition is built into the activities, teachers don't have to worry about fire drills, school pictures, or the flu. The game-intense structure and flexibility of the semester gives the entire class a feeling of spontaneity and venturesome exploration that most students find hard to resist — even if it means learning drama.

Do you really expect us to do all this?

Before you gasp, of course we don't expect you to rigidly follow everything in the book. We've included everything because it works for us. Use what is helpful to you; ignore the rest. Mix and match as suits your curriculum, but know that if you're ever in a pinch, a game you previously skipped might be just what you need. As both Justine and Mary Ann are cookbook junkies, we know about those substitutions made at the last minute and the old favorites that have the pages stuck together. We also know we'd never try every recipe in the book — just the ones that taste great in our minds' mouths. We won't hold it against you if you don't do everything we suggest. Neither of us has ever done a semester *exactly* as outlined.

We've provided over ninety days of lesson plans. This should give you enough to work with plus the flexibility to skip lessons you feel are redundant and linger over ones your players enjoy most.

I have to critique class work? The players are baring their souls! How should I do it?

Effectively critiquing student performances is an art form. One must tread a very fine line between encouragement and evaluation, especially with beginners. In our opinion, the first and foremost *raison d' être* is to *ensure that the performers feel comfortable performing*. If they feel that peers or the director are harshly judging them, all your hard work may be lost. On the other hand, only focusing on the positive may seem superficial.

We offer these few words of advice:

- When critiquing by peer or group leader, always start with what you *liked* about the performance, then go on to what can be improved.

- Balance the positives and negatives.

- Never allow overly eager peers to hurt feelings by making personal hurtful comments. ("You sucked!" "The others were better than Max." "It looked as if you didn't put any time into it," etc.)

- Practice wording comments sensitively. ("Melissa talks very softly, and it seemed to fit her character.")

- Avoid the "It was good, but ..." comment.

- Avoid generic comments. ("It was good. I liked it.")

- Focus on specifics. ("When Ellen jumped over the bench, it really showed me how terrified her character was.")

You will be amazed how quickly a group can adapt to making positive and constructive comments. What goes around really does come around!

How can I possibly grade improvs and games?

We personally dislike grades in a class meant to develop creativity. When students feel that they are being graded, they tend to focus on minutiae instead of letting the creativity flow. In young performers this usually takes the form of trying to be funny to get appreciative laughter from their peers.

However, since grades are a reality in most institutions of learning, we recommend that each exercise get a group and an individual grade. Be aware that some groups are higher functioning or more experienced than others. It is very difficult not to penalize a good performer if they happen to get into a weak group, and sometimes having the two grades doesn't even help. Usually there are so many exercises that a single poor grade is lost in the crowd.

Rubrics: Justine doesn't like them. Mary Ann does.

Self-Assessment: We find that this is often useless without a time-consuming instructional unit to precede it — especially with less mature students.

Kids do like to know what you are looking for, though, and an accurate answer to "What are we being graded on?" usually suffices.

What about kids who are shy or aren't team players?

The lessons are structured sequentially, building on skills learned over time. We place a great deal of emphasis and spend a lot of time on group building. Since most drama classes are made up of a wide variety of students, some eager and experienced, many not, we find that it is essential to create a classroom climate that is fun loving and non-judgmental. Indeed, our classes often feel like recreation time in that the learning is so holistic that the students often learn without being aware of it. At open house some parents remark that their student will most likely not be able to do well in the class, as they are too shy and/or do not like to perform. They beg us not to put their child on the spot. We agree. We also know that within a few days or weeks that very same student will be volunteering eagerly. It is all a matter of approach.

I know games; what do you mean by improv?

We mean **the impromptu creation of a scene with lines and action extemporized as the scene progresses.** Different directors allow varying degrees of preparation. The popular show, *Whose Line Is It, Anyway?* demands on-the-spot performances of very experienced professionals. An elementary language arts teacher may spend a significant amount of time discussing plot and character elements before improvising actual scenes. Improvisation may be performed before an understanding audience or before one director. It may be an end unto itself or the springboard of a finished product such as those of The Second City's *Story Theatre.*

How can I use improv?

Improv can be used as individual activities to fill time, as an instructional method to teach students dramatic concepts, and to introduce students to thinking creatively on their feet. As such we feel that improv is not only fun but also invaluable! Our students think so, too.

A fast pace contributes to the effectiveness of the activity. Keith Johnstone always says "Don't be prepared." This is extremely important to emphasize, as beginning players tend to feel that more careful planning makes for better scenes. We always stress that improv is a process, not an end in itself. As such, participation is the key factor, not being clever. There is a fine line between judging an improv successful as a performance and critiquing the process. In general, when the group is new, it is very important to focus on the process and applying what they learned in previous sessions rather than the product.

Are there improv guidelines?

Improv must be fun and non-threatening to succeed. Regardless of the methods or goals of specific improvisations, there are a few guidelines generally used:

- **Just do it.** Agree. Improv depends upon teamwork and playing off one another. Refusing to play or changing the ideas is called blocking and does not carry the improv forward.

- **Have fun.** Remember, improvs are a *fun* way to explore the abilities of one's self and fellow players, the group's dynamics, and theatre. Follow the rules, follow the time limits, and share with your partners. Relax and have a good time. Improvs are not judged — participation is.

- **Keep it appropriate.** Improv depends on everyone — participants and audience alike — having a good time without worrying about being offended or hurt. There should be no profanity, obscenity, inappropriate references, hurtful statements, or cruelty. Everyone participating should feel comfortable.

The appendix contains improv vocabulary that should help players understand the concepts (see page 200).

Those were guidelines for the players — what about for me?

The success of any game depends on the group and their reactions to it. Some games can go for the entire class period, and the students will beg to play them again the next day. Others may not work for your class, and you may want to shelve them for later or not at all. Depending on the length of your class period, how much time has been spent on other activities before the prepared one, and the size of your group, you may find yourself running out of performance or even preparatory time. We recommend that you do not extend performance into the next day's class, as the momentum drops off overnight. If you find yourself running out of time, either give the groups more preparatory time the next day or have one group demonstrate and critique that group fully for the entire class. Then all groups can start the next session fresh.

Any last words?

The structure of this curriculum has evolved over the years, and it has had to adapt to the ever-changing needs of the students, schools, and state and federal expectations. As any teacher knows, the group of students in period one will be very different from the students in period three (let alone period seven). You may finish a day's lesson in one class, but the same lesson may take several days in another class. An activity may fall flat with one group while it soars with another. Know yourself and your group. Do not try to fit a round peg into a square hole. It is up to the teacher/director/group leader to make lessons that fit the needs of the group on any specific day. If the day's lesson doesn't seem to be working, save it for another day and try something else. Most importantly, have fun! If you are having at least as much fun as your students, all will be well, and you'll have worthwhile educational experiences!

Break a leg!

Plot: A Beginning, a Middle, and an Ending

The beginning contains the *exposition* which establishes *who, where, when,* and *while.* Most improvisation requires that the information be delivered quickly and concisely. For improvs that start immediately, the first player must give as much information to fellow players as possible. The beginning ends with the *inciting incident* or introduction of the problem.

The middle contains the *rising action,* which is the action which leads up to a *crisis.* Longer improvs may have several crises, each followed by a reduction in dramatic intensity, or *falling action,* which then leads into another increase in intensity and crisis.

The ending contains the final crisis — the moment of greatest dramatic intensity — which is called the *climax.* Improvs often end immediately after the climax. They may, however, offer the resolution and tying up of loose ends afforded with a *denouement.*

Groups: What, How, and When

Group composition

How does one arrive at the subgroups for games? Changing subgroup composition allows players to work with people they might not work with otherwise, but how do we get groups that are comfortable and work well together to change? Here are a few of our tricks.

Choose your own group: This technique is great with new players. It adds a level of comfort to the often uncomfortable or threatening idea of improvisation.

Work with a group that has one person you haven't worked with before: Allowing players to work with some people who are familiar helps them to expand their working relationships to include others in the large group.

Number off: Simple, but it works. Decide on the size of the subgroups you need. Divide the total number of players by the number of players in a subgroup. Have players number off into the number of subgroups you need. Then all ones work together, all twos work together, etc. If there are remainders, have them work with a group of their choosing or your assignment.

Assign groups: Why not? Especially after the large group has worked for a while and you are familiar with the individual members' styles. This technique can lead to magic.

Group size

Most of the games in this book are written to accommodate a large group of twenty-four to forty players. More than that, and playing time with smaller subgroups becomes unwieldy; fewer than that, and there often aren't enough players to divide into larger subgroups. Subgroups are as few as one and as many as six. *These numbers are just suggestions*; individual directors may choose to use smaller or larger subgroups to accommodate their own large group and players' skills.

Performance order

"May we go first? Let us be first, oh, please!" We have discovered that deciding on performance order before the first improv leaves little room for anguish later. Eager volunteers to improv in front of the large group is music to any director's ears, but sorting through the volunteers can be as difficult as assigning reluctant players. Here are some tricks to try.

Volunteering: "Who wants to go first?" The first hand that pops up goes. "Next?" The next hand, and so forth. (Don't forget to write them down!)

Assigning: Alphabetically by last — or first — name of a group's representative. The first group to go was the last group in the previous improv.

Random: "Choose a number between one and twenty-five." Draw from facedown, numbered index cards. Draw numbered ping-pong balls from a paper bag.

Combination of techniques.

About the Daily Plans

Curriculums come in all shapes and sizes! Most of them contain long lists or cumbersome narratives that are often difficult or time consuming to absorb. For this reason we decided to do something different with ours. When we wrote *Improv Ideas*, we realized that it was a very useful tool. The games and lists are great when a teacher wants a quick idea ready-made. Several teachers, however, asked us how the games could be used in a classroom for something other than a rainy-day activity. "How in the world," they asked, "can you make an actual course out of these?" Well, here's the answer!

How it began

Justine has been teaching courses called Theatre Arts or Drama for over thirty years at both the high school and middle school levels. Most of these classes are semester-long introductions to theatre. She found that there was always a wide range of students in her classes. Some were quite experienced in acting while others were complete novices who needed to lose their fears of performing. In order to serve this wide range of needs, interests, and abilities, she found that she was using more and more improvisations and drama games and less lecture and formal script work. Amazingly, the interest level and participation soared! Eventually the classes became so popular that extra sessions were needed, and Mary Ann was hired to teach the overflow. Now the entire course is based around these games.

As a curriculum

This book could be called a curriculum or an activity guide. As a curriculum, it teaches basic theatre skills in a consecutive order, touching on the basics in acting, communication skills, group building, playmaking, playwriting, and critiquing.

As an activity guide

As an activity guide, each lesson includes specific games and activities used as a thematic unit of the day. The lesson's emphasis is clearly stated at the top of the lesson, and specific suggestions for how these games have worked in the classroom are included. Of course, individual teachers may mix and match, choosing to sequence the games within a lesson, or even the order of lessons, to fit his/her classes' needs.

Materials and equipment

Each day's lesson includes suggestions for materials and equipment. Typical classroom equipment such as chairs and desks are not listed, as we assume you will already have access to these on a daily basis.

Time

Please note that the time indicated for each game is approximate and geared to a sixty-minute class. You may vary this as you see fit. Also note that the times given on the game pages may vary. This it because the times for activities in the lesson plan section are the timelines for the entire activity, not for individual performances and preparation.

Organization

Take a look at the table of contents to get a sense for how the book is organized. Then glance through the sequence of the units and lessons, noting the titles of each day's lesson. Notice the flow from simple, group-based activities to more extensive projects incorporating many of the learned skills. Be aware that it is important to learn the basics before attempting more complex activities in order to avoid frustration.

The skills presented in this curriculum

Drama curriculums are often divided into goals and objectives, most of them focusing on the acquisition of specific skills. In *Improv Ideas* we linked all the games to the national theatre standards. In this book, we have divided the goals and objectives into thirty units. All of the activities address three broad categories of learning — drama/theatre, interpersonal, and personal — to some degree. We would hope that by the end of a semester, all students would be in the process of integrating these skills into their own lives and awareness and that they would carry over into all activities.

Because this curriculum may be used in many classroom settings, from upper elementary to beginning theatre in high school or college, we can't tell you just where your own students should be in their development. Look to your own state or department's objectives for that information.

Drama students should grow in the following areas:

Dramatic/Theatrical skills
- Adapt to endowments
- Communicate thoughts and feelings clearly
- Create mood through sound
- Create sets from simple objects
- Develop a scene with a beginning, a middle, and an ending
- Develop and sustain mood (suspense)
- Develop different characters for portrayal
- Express a range of characters
- Express a range of emotions
- Gather dramatic ideas from a variety of prompts
- Give and take focus
- Speak extemporaneously
- Understand and use role status
- Understand how plots and scenes need a beginning, a middle, and an ending
- Use beginning-middle-ending structures in improvisation
- Use drama's vocabulary to effectively communicate with others
- Use levels effectively
- Use objects symbolically
- Use props creatively
- Use stage areas effectively
- Use various styles/genres in improvised scenes
- Use voice and movement to create characters

Personal skills
- Accept constructive criticism
- Accept the contributions of others
- Appreciate diversity
- Be on task in a group
- Contribute ideas
- Critique knowledgeably and appropriately
- Develop and extend levels of concentration
- Empathize
- Evaluate own work
- Express own point of view
- Extend levels of concentration

- Increase amount and level of participation
- Increase confidence
- Make creative choices
- Participate as part of a group
- Perform solo
- Stay on task
- Think creatively
- Trust self
- Work in an ensemble

Interpersonal skills

- Be positive and supportive
- Be responsible to the group
- Compromise
- Design and perform an improvised group scene
- Experiment with ideas
- Finish dramatic group tasks
- Interact as an ensemble
- Listen to the contributions and opinions of others
- Make creative decisions collectively
- Pay attention to detail
- Respect diverse opinions
- Share ideas
- Trust the group
- Understand give-and-take in group performances

Lessons and Games

Breaking the Ice

Lesson 1: Getting Acquainted I

Emphasis: Playing well-known party games to break the ice.

Equipment: Stopwatch, paper

Hint: Try to start the sessions with the entire class involved in some sort of active movement as this energizes the group!

Line Up By Height   Minutes: 10
Silence is essential during many phases of rehearsal, playmaking, and class work. Plus, communicating nonverbally is a basis of ensemble acting.

Charades   Minutes: 30
Using this familiar party guessing game is a fun and non-threatening way to start dramatic activities.

I'm Going on a Trip   Minutes: 20
This game stimulates creativity while encouraging a fun atmosphere.

Lesson 2: Getting Acquainted II

May take 2 class periods

Emphasis: Learning about one another and the personality of the group.

Equipment: Key chains, chairs, stool

Hint: *Truth or Lie?* can go on for two class periods, depending on the time available and the enthusiasm of the group. Time can also be spent analyzing how people present themselves differently when they are lying or telling the truth. Try starting each new session with one true tall tale.

Fruit Basket Upset   Minutes: 15-20
Playing games together can help us learn more about the personality of the group.

Key Chains   Minutes: 15
Deductions, both general and specific, can be made based on close observation.

Truth or Lie?   Minutes: 20-30
"Tall tales" can be true or false.

Line Up by Height

DEMO
0
MINUTES

PLAYER PREP
0
MINUTES

PERFORMANCE
10
MINUTES

Discuss

- The importance of silence in many aspects of theatre.
- The importance of communicating nonverbally (with no sounds).

Directions

- The director indicates where the beginning and end of the line should be.
- The group lines up quickly and silently by height.

Focus Questions

- Did natural leaders emerge?
- How were conflicts resolved nonverbally?
- Was it accomplished without noise?

Variations

- Line up chromatically by shirt color.
- Line up by hair color.

And after the group gets to know each other:
- Line up by first name.
- Line up by last name.

Type: Whole group
Skill: Beginning
Group Size: Whole group
Equipment: None

We play this game because:

Silence is essential during many phases of rehearsal, playmaking, and class work. Plus, communicating nonverbally is a basis of ensemble acting.

Emphasis:

Blocking and Conventions
Characterization
Concentration
Creativity
Ensemble Acting
Following Directions
Give and Take Focus
Group Dynamics
Listening and Silence
Memorization
Nonverbal Communication
Observation
Physical Control
Plot Structure
Spontaneity
Storytelling

Try this game again toward the end of the semester. The growth in how the group works together is usually phenomenal and very gratifying.

Charades

DEMO
0
MINUTES

PLAYER PREP
0
MINUTES

PERFORMANCE
2
MINUTES

Type: Whole group
Skill: Beginning
Group Size: Whole group
Equipment: Watch with second hand or stopwatch, slips of paper with the word/words and the category written on them and folded in half

We play this game because:
Precise physical presence conveys meaning without words.

Emphasis:

Blocking and Conventions

Characterization

Concentration

Creativity

Ensemble Acting

Following Directions

Give and Take Focus

Group Dynamics

Listening and Silence

Memorization

Nonverbal Communication

Observation

Physical Control

Plot Structure

Spontaneity

Storytelling

Discuss

The rules of Charades (see appendix page 202).

Directions

- The director chooses a reliable timekeeper and sets a two-minute time limit.
- The first volunteer goes to the front of the group and selects a word or phrase to be acted out.
- The group guesses the word or phrase based on the volunteer's pantomime.
- If the word/phrase is not guessed within two minutes, the timekeeper calls "Stop," and the word/phrase is divulged.

Focus Questions

- What made the word or phrase easy to guess?
- Did you see any extraneous gestures that confused you or made it hard to guess?
- How can playing *Charades* improve our drama performances?

You can find a helpful list in *Improv Ideas*:
Famous People — Page 59
Clichés (and Tired Phrases) —
Pages 29-31

I'm Going on a Trip

DEMO	PLAYER PREP	PERFORMANCE
0 MINUTES	**0** MINUTES	**20** MINUTES

Directions

- Players sit in a circle.
- The first player begins the story with "I'm going on a trip, and I'm taking a/an _____(Object that begins with the letter 'a')." The player must choose an object that can be taken on a trip.
- The next player in the circle repeats the phrase "I'm going on a trip, and I'm taking a _____ (object that begins with a 'b')," and then adds the first player's object.
- The third player starts with a new object that beings with a "c" then adds the second actor's object then the first actor's object.

Example

- I'm going on a trip, and I'm taking an apple.
- I'm going on a trip and I'm taking a baseball bat and an apple.
- I'm going on a trip and I'm taking my cat, a baseball bat, and an apple.

Focus Questions

- Which items were the hardest to remember?
- Did you use any tricks to help you memorize? Share them with the group.

Challenge the Players to Ramp it Up!

- Go around the circle more than once.
- Speed up the process. Allow no more than a set number of seconds for players to respond.

Type: Whole group
Skill: Beginning
Group Size: Whole group
Equipment: None

We play this game because:

This game stimulates creativity while encouraging memorization in a fun atmosphere.

Emphasis:

Blocking and Conventions

Characterization

Concentration

Creativity

Ensemble Acting

Following Directions

Give and Take Focus

Group Dynamics

Listening and Silence

Memorization

Nonverbal Communication

Observation

Physical Control

Plot Structure

Spontaneity

Storytelling

Make sure that everyone sees this game as just for fun. Help players who can't remember. Start over when things bog down.

Fruit Basket Upset

DEMO
0
MINUTES

PLAYER PREP
0
MINUTES

PERFORMANCE
15+
MINUTES

Type: Whole group
Skill: Beginning
Group Size: Whole group
Equipment: Chairs for all but one player

We play this game because:

Playing games together can help us learn more about the personality of the group.

Emphasis:

Blocking and Conventions

Characterization

Concentration

Creativity

Ensemble Acting

Following Directions

Give and Take Focus

Group Dynamics

Listening and Silence

Memorization

Nonverbal Communication

Observation

Physical Control

Plot Structure

Spontaneity

Storytelling

Directions

- All players — except one who stands — sit on chairs in a circle.
- The person standing calls out a category. All players who feel they fit in the category get up and switch seats. They may not sit one chair on either side of where they were last seated.
- Once everyone has moved, one person will be without a seat. That person calls out the next category.
- The play continues.

Focus Questions

- What were some things the majority of the group has in common?
- What things only affected a very few?
- Could you make some general statements about the makeup of the group based on their responses to the categories in the game?

This game is one of the absolute best "getting to know you" activities we know! You can find a helpful list in *Improv Ideas*: Categories — Page 21

Key Chains

DEMO
0
MINUTES

PLAYER PREP
0
MINUTES

PERFORMANCE
15
MINUTES

Directions

- Group sits on floor in front of displayed key chain collection.
- Players get five minutes to look at individual key chains by moving to different areas of the chain every minute.
- At the end of the five minutes, the director asks the students to make some deductions about the owner of the collection based on at least three key chains.
- Discussion ensues about how inferences can be made based on observations.

Examples

- Three key chains from different countries could mean that the owner likes to travel.
- Three Disney key chains could mean that the owner likes cartoon characters.
- Three key chains with a certain name on them could mean that the owner has a loved one by that name.

Focus Questions

- How did you categorize the key chains?
- What kind of deductions did you make?
- What is the difference between a general deduction and one that is more specific?
- What is a faulty deduction? How is a faulty deduction made?

Type: Whole group
Skill: Beginning
Group Size: Whole group
Equipment: Key chains

We play this game because:
Deductions, both general and specific, can be made based on close observation.

Emphasis:

Blocking and Conventions

Characterization

Concentration

Creativity

Ensemble Acting

Following Directions

Give and Take Focus

Group Dynamics

Listening and Silence

Memorization

Nonverbal Communication

Observation

Physical Control

Plot Structure

Spontaneity

Storytelling

Note: We play this game with Justine's key chain collection, which is presently forty-two feet long. We recommend that you have a chain of key chains at least three feet long before you play this game. This can also be played with objects in a purse, wallet, or backpack.

Truth or Lie?

DEMO
5
MINUTES

PLAYER PREP
0
MINUTES

PERFORMANCE
20+
MINUTES

Type: Whole group
Skill: Beginning
Group Size: Whole group
Equipment: Stool

We play this game because:
"Tall tales" can be true or false.

Emphasis:

Blocking and Conventions

Characterization

Concentration

Creativity

Ensemble Acting

Following Directions

Give and Take Focus

Group Dynamics

Listening and Silence

Memorization

Nonverbal Communication

Observation

Physical Control

Plot Structure

Spontaneity

Storytelling

Directions

- A stool is placed in front of the group.
- The director models this game by volunteering a story to be judged "truth or lie" by the group.
- Stories are then shared by volunteers from the group and judged "truth or lie."

Examples

- The director tells the story behind a shark key ring. She tells about a shark attack aborted by a teacher at the school where she taught. The class judges it a lie. It was true!
- A student tells a story about being caught in a huge wave and being swept a mile out to sea. The class judges it true. It is a lie.

Focus Questions

- How were the stories constructed to have a beginning, a middle, and an ending?
- How was the conflict/climax added or incorporated?
- How did you tell the difference between a truth and a lie? (Eye contact, pauses, too many/too few details, etc.)
- Did the group guess more truths or lies?
- Were there differences in content/style between truths and lies?

It always helps to have prompts for the stories. These may be key chains, postcards, or even a personal scar!

Unit 2:
The Group Emerges

Lesson 3: Learning Names

Emphasis: Focusing on learning names and working together.

Equipment: A ball

Hint: Not being — or allowing players to be — critical when players "mess up" is essential to creating an open and creative atmosphere for the rest of the semester.

Name Game   **Minutes: 20**
Getting to know the people in the group is often easier when you can make associations.

Name Ball   **Minutes: 15**
Sounds can help propel movement across distances.

You!   **Minutes: 15-20**
Keeping a fast pace with few, if any, breaks keeps interest up and momentum going.

Lesson 4: Working as a Group

Emphasis: Working together and following directions as a group.

Equipment: Chairs

Hint: Always be aware of the group's ability to keep standing. If they tire easily, insert *Frog and Fly* in the middle for a rest, as this is a sitting game.

Simon Says   **Minutes: 10**
Intense concentration is needed to follow instructions that are given rapidly and/or in a confusing manner.

Who Started the Motion?   **Minutes: 15**
Working together as a group is the beginning of ensemble acting.

Frog and Fly   **Minutes: 20-30**
Working together as a group can benefit the outcome of the game and of a scene.

Name Game

DEMO
0
MINUTES

PLAYER PREP
0
MINUTES

PERFORMANCE
15+
MINUTES

Type: Whole group
Skill: Beginning
Group Size: Whole group
Equipment: None

We play this game because:

Getting to know the people in the group is often easier when you can make associations.

Emphasis:

Blocking and Conventions
Characterization
Concentration
Creativity
Ensemble Acting
Following Directions
Give and Take Focus
Group Dynamics
Listening and Silence
Memorization
Nonverbal Communication
Observation
Physical Control
Plot Structure
Spontaneity
Storytelling

Directions

- Players sit in a circle. The director decides the size of the circle or how often the process restarts.
- The director encourages the players to think of a friendly but accurate adjective that describes them and starts with the same sound as their first names.
- The director chooses a player to start. The first player says, "I'm (own name), and I'm (character trait)."
- The next player says, "I'm (own name), and I'm (character trait). S/he's (first player's name), and s/he's (first player's character trait)."
- This continues around the circle with the players saying their own names and appropriate character traits and reciting the names and character traits of all players who went before them.

Focus Questions

- Did anyone have a hard time thinking of an adjective to describe themselves?
- Was this because of the letter of the alphabet, the fact that the word you wanted had already been used, or did you just not know how to describe yourself?
- Was it easier to remember people's names by associating them with the adjectives?

Challenge Players to Ramp It Up!!

Add a physical element — anything from a gesture to a full-body movement that expresses the character trait.

The director's job includes making players comfortable with the game and downplaying memorization.
You can find a helpful list in *Improv Ideas*: Character Traits — Pages 24-27

Name Ball

DEMO
0
MINUTES

PLAYER PREP
0
MINUTES

PERFORMANCE
10+
MINUTES

Directions

- Group stands in a circle.
- One player throws a ball and says his/her name.
- Another player catches the ball and says his/her name as he/she throws the ball to another player.
- The game continues until all players have received and thrown the ball at least once.
- Take care to throw the ball easily so no one is hurt and the ball is easy to catch.

Focus Questions

- Why was it important to keep the ball going?
- Was it easy or difficult to remember the players' names after doing this activity?
- Was it easier to say your name or make a sound? Why?

Type: Whole group
Skill: Beginning
Group Size: Whole group
Equipment: A ball

We play this game because:
Sounds can help propel movement across distances.

Emphasis:

Blocking and Conventions

Characterization

Concentration

Creativity

Ensemble Acting

Following Directions

Give and Take Focus

Group Dynamics

Listening and Silence

Memorization

Nonverbal Communication

Observation

Physical Control

Plot Structure

Spontaneity

Storytelling

Catching is sometimes an issue. Downplay athletic ability so everyone feels comfortable.

You!

Type: Whole group
Skill: Beginning
Group Size: Whole group
Equipment: None

We play this game because:

Keeping a fast pace with few, if any, breaks keeps interest up and momentum going.

Emphasis:

Blocking and Conventions
Characterization
Concentration
Creativity
Ensemble Acting
Following Directions
Give and Take Focus
Group Dynamics
Listening and Silence
Memorization
Nonverbal Communication
Observation
Physical Control
Plot Structure
Spontaneity
Storytelling

Directions

- The group stands in a circle.
- One player extends an arm, points to another player in the circle, and says, "You!" He/She starts to walk toward the other player with the intention of taking that player's place.
- The player who was pointed at immediately points at another player, says, "You!" and starts to take that player's place.
- Players cross each other in the center as they take their new places.
- When rhythm has been established and the group feels comfortable with the games, add another word, such as the name of a food or a color.
- Try to keep three words going simultaneously (like juggling words and movement rather than balls).
- Remember that there may be up to six players crossing at one time if you are using a "You!", a color, and a food.
- If the group is really good, try adding even more.

Focus Questions

- Why was it important to keep the pace going?
- Why did extending the arm help move you forward?
- Was it difficult to think of words under pressure?
- Was it difficult to keep more than one word going? Why?

You! requires very tight concentration. See how many words the group can do at one time. You can find a helpful list in *Improv Ideas*: Categories — Page 21

Simon Says

DEMO
0
MINUTES

PLAYER PREP
0
MINUTES

PERFORMANCE
5+
MINUTES

Directions

- Players stand in a circle.
- One player is selected to be Simon.
- Simon is to always preface his instructions with the words, "Simon says" (Example: "Simon says clap your hands").
- Once the group gets a momentum going, Simon will try to change motions rapidly.
- Once the group is capable of changing rapidly, Simon may try to trick them into doing movements not prefaced with "Simon says."
- Individuals who do a motion that was not prefaced by "Simon says" are out.
- Play continues until most of the players are out.

Focus Questions

- How difficult was it to follow directions when they were given rapidly?
- What did you do to concentrate on what was being said?
- Did Simon use any techniques to trick the group? What were they? Why did they work?

Type: Whole group
Skill: Beginning
Group Size: Whole group
Equipment: None

We play this game because:

Intense concentration is needed to follow instructions that are given rapidly and/or in a confusing manner.

Emphasis:

Blocking and Conventions

Characterization

Concentration

Creativity

Ensemble Acting

Following Directions

Give and Take Focus

Group Dynamics

Listening and Silence

Memorization

Nonverbal Communication

Observation

Physical Control

Plot Structure

Spontaneity

Storytelling

Stress to Simon leaders that movements should be simple.

Who Started the Motion?

DEMO
0
MINUTES

PLAYER PREP
0
MINUTES

PERFORMANCE
10+
MINUTES

Type: Whole group
Skill: Beginning
Group Size: Whole group
Equipment: None

We play this game because:

Working together as a group is the beginning of ensemble acting.

Emphasis:

Blocking and Conventions

Characterization

Concentration

Creativity

Ensemble Acting

Following Directions

Give and Take Focus

Group Dynamics

Listening and Silence

Memorization

Nonverbal Communication

Observation

Physical Control

Plot Structure

Spontaneity

Storytelling

Directions

- Players stand in a circle.
- One player is "It" and leaves the room.
- The director chooses a leader to start a simple motion (clapping hands, stamping feet, swinging arms, etc.). All other players do the exact motion as the leader.
- The leader must change the motion frequently. The director allows the group to work together for a short while, stressing that all players need to follow the leader closely without obviously watching the leader.
- It returns, comes to the middle of the circle, and watches the motions carefully.
- It gets three guesses as to which player is leader.
- After It has guessed correctly or used up all of his guesses, another person is chosen to be It, and the play continues.

Focus Questions

- What strategies did the group use to observe when the movement changed?
- How did the group's reaction affect the guessing?
- Were there mistakes made by the leader (changing while It was watching) or the group (not paying enough attention and forgetting to change)? How did these affect the guessing?
- How did It guess correctly?

Remind players to keep the motions simple and broad enough for everyone to see.

Frog and Fly

Directions

- Group sits in a circle.
- One Player is chosen to be "It" and leaves the room.
- One player is chosen to be "Frog." The remaining players are flies.
- When Frog sticks out his tongue, the fly to whom the tongue appears to be directed must fall to the ground, make a dying scene, and lie still.
- It is brought back into the room, goes to the center of the circle, watches flies "die," and gets three guesses as to which player is Frog.
- This game is similar to *Who Started the Motion?* The object for Frog is to "kill" as many flies as possible without being caught. The object for It is to discover who Frog is.

Focus Questions

- How did It guess who was the Frog?
- How did Frog trick It?
- How did the flies trick It?
- Were the death scenes energetic?
- What made the game fun?
- How did group cooperation help trick It?

Type: Whole group
Skill: Beginning
Group Size: Whole group
Equipment: Chairs for the group

We play this game because:

Working together as a group can benefit the outcome of the game and of a scene.

Emphasis:

Blocking and Conventions

Characterization

Concentration

Creativity

Ensemble Acting

Following Directions

Give and Take Focus

Group Dynamics

Listening and Silence

Memorization

Nonverbal Communication

Observation

Physical Control

Plot Structure

Spontaneity

Storytelling

This is one of the most popular games for elementary and middle school students. They love to die in agony.

Look What We Can Do

Lesson 5: Vocal Stretching

Emphasis: Conveying meaning and emotions through vocal variety.

Equipment: Newspapers, a ball

Hint: Let the players be as corny as they want. Go crazy! Have fun!

Newsies   Minutes: 10-15
Spontaneously reading headlines to create interest can result in vocal stretching.

Hi, How Are You?   Minutes: 10-15
Our voices carry meaning no matter how clichéd our words might be.

Sound Ball   Minutes: 15-20
When players have to make up sounds "on the spot," interesting noises occur. Anything goes!

Lesson 6: Following Directions

Emphasis: Working together following directions.

Equipment: Chairs, swimming noodles

Hint: Cooperation is the beginning of ensemble work! Passing is *not* an option.

Poop Deck   Minutes: 15-20
Following the director's instructions is critical when rehearsing a play.

Telephone   Minutes: 15-20
Listening closely is essential.

One-Sentence-at-a-Time Story   Minutes: 15
"Just do it" is important advice for getting the creative juices flowing.

Newsies

DEMO 0 MINUTES

PLAYER PREP 0 MINUTES

PERFORMANCE 10+ MINUTES

Directions

- Newspapers are spread out on the floor of the room.
- Players also spread out across the room.
- When the director gives the signal, players move about the room shouting headlines aloud simultaneously in the emotion suggested by the headline.

Examples

- "Bat Boy Escapes," as if shocked.
- "Polar Bear Gives Birth to Triplets," as if excited.
- "Car Crash Kills Two," as if saddened.
- "Hurricane Donations Needed," as if urgent.
- "Gas Prices Soar," as if angered.

Focus Questions

- Were you able to express the headlines in different emotions?
- Were there many emotional responses suggested by the headlines?
- Could you concentrate while others were also emoting?

Type: Whole group
Skill: Beginning
Group Size: Whole group
Equipment: Newspapers

We play this game because:
Spontaneously reading headlines to create interest can result in vocal stretching.

Emphasis:

Blocking and Conventions

Characterization

Concentration

Creativity

Ensemble Acting

Following Directions

Give and Take Focus

Group Dynamics

Listening and Silence

Memorization

Nonverbal Communication

Observation

Physical Control

Plot Structure

Spontaneity

Storytelling

The director should be prepared with a variety of emotional reactions to help the players.

Hi, How Are You?

DEMO
5
MINUTES

PLAYER PREP
0
MINUTES

PERFORMANCE
5+
MINUTES

Type: Whole group
Skill: Beginning
Group Size: Whole group
Equipment: None

We play this game because:

Our voices carry meaning no matter how clichéd our words might be.

Emphasis:

Blocking and Conventions
Characterization
Concentration
Creativity
Ensemble Acting
Following Directions
Give and Take Focus
Group Dynamics
Listening and Silence
Memorization
Nonverbal Communication
Observation
Physical Control
Plot Structure
Spontaneity
Storytelling

Directions

- The players stand or sit in a circle.
- The first player turns to the player on his/her left and says, "Hi, how are you?"
- The second player responds, "I'm fine. Thank you."
- The second player then turns to the player on his/her left and says, "Hi, how are you?"
- The object of the game is to keep mini-conversations going, but to do each exchange in a different vocal tone.
- When a conversation is said in the same vocal tone as a previous conversation, the player goes into the middle (mush pot) or is out.

Examples

- "Hi, how are you?" said as if concerned.
- "I'm fine. Thank you," said as if annoyed.
- "Hi, how are you?" said as if flirting.
- "I'm fine. Thank you," said as if angry.

Focus Questions

- What were the "conversations" about? Give some examples.
- How did changes in vocal tone, stress, etc., affect the interpretation of the words?
- Did facial expressions and gestures help the interpretation?
- Was it difficult to change the interpretation?
- Did the words limit the emotional content?

Ask players to recall times from earlier in the day when they had this conversation and discuss.

Sound Ball

DEMO
2
MINUTES

PLAYER PREP
0
MINUTES

PERFORMANCE
5+
MINUTES

Directions

- Players stand in a circle.
- Player One throws a ball across the circle to Player Two.
- As Player One throws the ball, she makes a sound.
- Player Two catches the ball and makes another sound while he throws the ball to a third player.
- Players keep the ball moving with sounds.

Examples

- Player One throws the ball with a roar.
- Player Two throws the ball with an evil laugh.
- Player Three throws the ball with a whoosh.
- Player Four throws the ball with a bark.
- Player Five throws the ball with a groan.

Focus Questions

- Was it difficult to think of sounds quickly?
- Were the sounds varied?
- Were the sounds creative?

Type: Whole group
Skill: Beginning
Group Size: Whole group
Equipment: A ball

We play this game because:
When players have to make up sounds "on the spot," interesting noises occur. Anything goes!

Emphasis:

Blocking and Conventions

Characterization

Concentration

Creativity

Ensemble Acting

Following Directions

Give and Take Focus

Group Dynamics

Listening and Silence

Memorization

Nonverbal Communication

Observation

Physical Control

Plot Structure

Spontaneity

Storytelling

A variation of *Sound Ball* is *Word Ball* — categories (foods, animals, names, etc.) are used instead of sounds.

Poop Deck

DEMO
0
MINUTES

PLAYER PREP
0
MINUTES

PERFORMANCE
15+
MINUTES

Type: Whole group
Skill: Beginning
Group Size: Whole group
Equipment: Clear the room or play outdoors, markers for the edges of the different decks (swimming noodles work well)

We play this game because:

Following the director's instructions quickly and accurately is critical when rehearsing a play.

Emphasis:

Blocking and Conventions
Characterization
Concentration
Creativity
Ensemble Acting
Following Directions
Give and Take Focus
Group Dynamics
Listening and Silence
Memorization
Nonverbal Communication
Observation
Physical Control
Plot Structure
Spontaneity
Storytelling

Directions

- The group lines up in front of the director.
- The director explains that Stage Right is the poop deck, Center Stage is the main deck, and Stage Left is the foredeck.
- The director or a volunteer also demonstrates the following instructions: "Scrub the deck" (on hands and knees scrubbing), "Man overboard" (swimming), "Captain! My Captain" (saluting), and "Boom" (falling flat on the deck).
- The play begins with the director calling out directions (example: "Man overboard on the Poop Deck!"). As in *Simon Says*, the director may give visually confusing directions. When players move the wrong way or respond too slowly, they are out.
- The play ends when there is one player remaining.
- The last player remaining is now the captain and takes the place of the director.

Focus Questions

- Why was it difficult to follow instructions?
- How did the captain psych you out?
- What techniques did you use to concentrate?

This game can get really lively; monitor action and caution players so they won't get hurt.

Telephone

DEMO
0
MINUTES

PLAYER PREP
0
MINUTES

PERFORMANCE
15+
MINUTES

Directions

- The group sits in a circle.
- The two players seated directly across from the director are designated tellers.
- The director whispers a short sentence to the persons on her left and right. (Examples: "Today I am excited because it's my birthday!" "I love to watch *I Love Lucy* reruns on TV.")
- The sentences are passed around the circle by whispering to the next players.
- When the message has been passed to the tellers, each teller tells the entire group the message.
- The game resumes with a new message.

Focus Questions

- Where do you think the message was changed? Why?
- Was it important that the person passing the message spoke clearly?
- How difficult was it to enunciate?

Type: Whole group
Skill: Beginning
Group Size: Whole group
Equipment: None

We play this game because:
Listening closely is an essential drama skill.

Emphasis:

Blocking and Conventions
Characterization
Concentration
Creativity
Ensemble Acting
Following Directions
Give and Take Focus
Group Dynamics
Listening and Silence
Memorization
Nonverbal Communication
Observation
Physical Control
Plot Structure
Spontaneity
Storytelling

Since most people know this game, make sure the players know they cannot say "operator" and have the message repeated.

One-Sentence-at-a-Time Story

DEMO
0
MINUTES

PLAYER PREP
0
MINUTES

PERFORMANCE
15
MINUTES

Type: Whole group
Skill: Beginning
Group Size: Whole group
Equipment: Chairs

We play this game because:
"Just do it" is important for getting the creative juices flowing.

Emphasis:

Blocking and Conventions

Characterization

Concentration

Creativity

Ensemble Acting

Following Directions

Give and Take Focus

Group Dynamics

Listening and Silence

Memorization

Nonverbal Communication

Observation

Physical Control

Plot Structure

Spontaneity

Storytelling

Directions

- Group sits in a circle.
- Director starts a story with a sentence. (Examples: "When I was sick I had a dream about marshmallows." "After the tornado I discovered frogs in my basement ... very unusual frogs." Etc.)
- Each player adds another sentence to the story in turn.
- The story should go around the circle once or twice depending on the size of the group.
- The story should be grammatically correct and contain a beginning, a middle, and an ending with a conflict or two.
- Keep up the pace. No passing.

Focus Questions

- Was it difficult to think of a plot?
- Was it difficult to choose words?
- Was it difficult to remember the correct part of speech?
- Did the story end too quickly?
- Did the story get bogged down in too many exaggerated details?
- Was it hard to end the story?

Challenge Players to Ramp It Up!

Play One-*Word*-at-a-Time!

Don't be too picky about grammar, but make sure the story has a coherent plot with a beginning, a middle, and an ending.

Quietly

Lesson 7: Nonverbal Sensing

Emphasis: Focusing on the senses and how we can use them to express ourselves.

Equipment: Blindfolds

Hint: Sometimes it is difficult spending an entire session without speaking. If you find this to be the case, be sure to incorporate discussion between each activity!

Sensing	**Minutes: 15**

Actors use all five senses to create complete characters.

As If ...	**Minutes: 15**

Group pantomime focuses on the physical without having to concentrate on dialog or character interactions and without worrying about the scrutiny of others.

Blind Walk	**Minutes: 30**

When we cannot see, we become more reliant on our other senses and, in this case, our trust in others.

Lesson 8: Nonverbal Communication

Emphasis: Working together and following directions with a focus on the nonverbal.

Equipment: None

Hint: When beginning pantomime work, stress having fun rather than being really precise in the movements.

Duck, Duck, Goose	**Minutes: 15-20**

Creativity and variety of pace and movement are important acting skills.

Walking	**Minutes: 15**

Emotions and environmental conditions affect how we walk.

It Ain't Heavy, It's ...	**Minutes: 15**

Working together to pantomime carrying objects that require concentration.

Sensing

DEMO 0 MINUTES

PLAYER PREP 0 MINUTES

PERFORMANCE 15 MINUTES

Type: Whole group
Skill: Beginning
Group Size: Whole group
Equipment: None

We play this game because:
Actors use all five senses to create complete characters.

Emphasis:

Blocking and Conventions

Characterization

Concentration

Creativity

Ensemble Acting

Following Directions

Give and Take Focus

Group Dynamics

Listening and Silence

Memorization

Nonverbal Communication

Observation

Physical Control

Plot Structure

Spontaneity

Storytelling

Directions
- Each member of the group finds a spot on the floor, or pairs sit in a circle with backs to each other.
- The director turns off all lights and ambient sounds in the room if possible.
- The players close their eyes.
- The director creates a scenario to which the players react using their senses. The director may concentrate on one sensory category or choose a few from each.
- The director asks each player to react nonverbally to the stated sensory stimuli. Players should try to use their entire bodies while reacting.

Examples
- All five senses: You are in a fancy restaurant ordering an exotic dinner. The waiter brings you a covered platter, opens the top, and you see and smell a very strange food with long tentacles. You start to pick it up, but it's squishy, and you drop it. Getting your fork, you wrap it around the fork and bring it to your mouth, savoring the exotic smell. Putting it in your mouth, you try to chew, but its rubbery texture makes it very difficult. You try to swallow, but it won't go down.
- Visual only: You are on the observation deck of a very tall building. Peering down, you see shadowy shapes below, seemingly running. Suddenly, a gigantic ape lumbers across your line of vision, picks up a shape (which you now identify as human), and eats it. The ape looks grotesque as he munches on his victim.

Focus Questions
- Was it difficult to quickly adapt to new cues?
- Which senses were the easiest for you to execute? Which were the most difficult?
- Did you feel limited by not being able to vocalize?

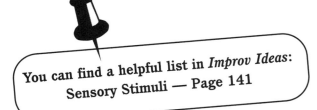

You can find a helpful list in *Improv Ideas*: Sensory Stimuli — Page 141

As If ...

DEMO
0
MINUTES

PLAYER PREP
0
MINUTES

PERFORMANCE
5
MINUTES

Directions

- The entire group spreads out across the room.
- The director instructs them to perform a pantomime "as if ..."
- After thirty seconds to a minute, the director changes the pantomime.
- This activity continues for about five minutes or until the group loses focus.
- Repeat the activity with a different pantomime theme.

Examples

- In the same emotion: watching a sad movie; writing a Dear John letter; writing and mailing a letter; taking the SAT.
- In chronological order: hiking in the woods, climbing a hill, picking up sticks, and building a campfire.

Focus Questions

- Which pantomimes were easiest for you? Why?
- Was it hard to switch focus?

Challenge Players to Ramp It Up!

- Develop a scene based on one of the pantomimes.
- Develop a scene incorporating *all* of the pantomimes.
- Stop the action and have the group focus on a particularly good example.

You can find a helpful list in *Improv Ideas*:
Pantomime Ideas — Page 111

Type: Whole group
Skill: Beginning
Group Size: Whole group
Equipment: None

We play this game because:

Group pantomimes focus on the physical without having to concentrate on dialog or character interactions and without having to worry about the scrutiny of others.

Emphasis:

Blocking and Conventions
Characterization
Concentration
Creativity
Ensemble Acting
Following Directions
Give and Take Focus
Group Dynamics
Listening and Silence
Memorization
Nonverbal Communication
Observation
Physical Control
Plot Structure
Spontaneity
Storytelling

Blind Walk

Type: Whole group
Skill: Intermediate
Group Size: 2
Equipment: Blindfolds, if desired

We play this game because:

When we cannot see, we become more reliant on our other senses and, in this case, our trust of others.

Emphasis:

Blocking and Conventions

Characterization

Concentration

Creativity

Ensemble Acting

Following Directions

Give and Take Focus

Group Dynamics

Listening and Silence

Memorization

Nonverbal Communication

Observation

Physical Control

Plot Structure

Spontaneity

Storytelling

Directions

- Group divides into pairs; each pair has Player A and Player B.
- Player A closes his eyes, and Player B leads Player A on a blind walk.
- Player B cannot touch Player A, but must instruct Player A where to move by the sound of her voice, her directions, and her proximity to Player A.
- Player B must take care to guide very carefully. It is a good idea to avoid stairs, stage edges, and levels if possible.
- Halfway through the agreed time, Player A becomes Player B's leader.
- When finished, all the pairs return to discuss the experience.

Focus Questions

- Was it difficult to trust the person leading you?
- Were the directions clear? If not, what would have helped?
- What were your fears?
- How did you experience moving while being unable to see?
- Did you notice anything new about your surroundings?
- Did you notice anything new about your own responses?

Be certain to stress that the leader must be very, very careful and must pay close attention to his/her blind partner's reactions so as to alleviate fear and inspire trust.

Duck, Duck, Goose

DEMO 0 MINUTES   **PLAYER PREP** 0 MINUTES   **PERFORMANCE** 15+ MINUTES

Directions

- Group sits on the floor in a circle.
- One player is chosen to be "It."
- It goes around the circle, tapping each player gently on the head, and saying either "duck" or "goose."
- Most of the taps will be "duck," which means that the tapped players stay where they are.
- When a player is tapped with "goose," he must jump up and try to tag It before It runs all the way around the circle and sits in Goose's original place.
- If Goose does not get back to his place before tagging It, then Goose is It.

Focus Questions

- Which types of movement were the easiest to use for chasing?
- What types were the most difficult?

Challenge Players to Ramp It Up!

Goose and It both race around the circle with a specific type of movement (skipping, hopping, walking backwards, etc.).

Caution: Players can get so revved up that they fall!

Type: Whole group
Skill: Beginning
Group Size: Whole group
Equipment: None

We play this game because:

Variety of pace and movement is an important acting skill.

Emphasis:

Blocking and Conventions
Characterization
Concentration
Creativity
Ensemble Acting
Following Directions
Give and Take Focus
Group Dynamics
Listening and Silence
Memorization
Nonverbal Communication
Observation
Physical Control
Plot Structure
Spontaneity
Storytelling

Walking

DEMO 0 MINUTES | PLAYER PREP 0 MINUTES | PERFORMANCE 10+ MINUTES

Type: Whole group
Skill: Beginning
Group Size: Whole group
Equipment: None

We play this game because:
Emotions and environmental conditions affect how we walk.

Emphasis:

Blocking and Conventions
Characterization
Concentration
Creativity
Ensemble Acting
Following Directions
Give and Take Focus
Group Dynamics
Listening and Silence
Memorization
Nonverbal Communication
Observation
Physical Control
Plot Structure
Spontaneity
Storytelling

Directions

- The players spread out around the room.
- The director calls different walks.
- Without any talking or physical contact, the players move about the space in the different types of walks.

Focus Questions

- Could you feel the physical tension in your body?
- Could you feel physical differences with the different types of walks?
- Which types of movement were most familiar to you?
- Which were the easiest to execute?

You can find a helpful list in *Improv Ideas*: Walks — Pages 165-167

It Ain't Heavy, It's ...

DEMO
5
MINUTES

PLAYER PREP
0
MINUTES

PERFORMANCE
10
MINUTES

Directions

- Group spreads out around the room in pairs.
- About every ten seconds the director calls out types of objects for the pairs to carry.
- Pairs pantomime carrying these objects, showing the shape, weight, and texture.

Examples

- A loaded coffin
- A wet dog
- A set of dishes
- A bass fiddle
- A car engine

Focus Questions

- Were different weights shown? How?
- Were different textures shown? How?
- Were different shapes shown? How?
- Were both players equally involved?
- Did you as a player feel physical tension?
- Did you feel differences in your body as the objects changed?
- Did your face need to be involved?

Type: Whole group
Skill: Beginning
Group Size: Whole group
Equipment: None

We play this game because:
Working together to pantomime carrying objects requires concentration.

Emphasis:

Blocking and Conventions

Characterization

Concentration

Creativity

Ensemble Acting

Following Directions

Give and Take Focus

Group Dynamics

Listening and Silence

Memorization

Nonverbal Communication

Observation

Physical Control

Plot Structure

Spontaneity

Storytelling

Try actually lifting objects of different weights and discussing how players' muscles are used with each object.

Physical Control

Lesson 9: Physicalization I

Emphasis: Accentuating other senses by focusing on activities that limit one or more sense.

Equipment: Blindfolds

Hint: Get ready for electricity! The focus in the group is almost palpable when you play these games.

Mirror Game   Minutes: 15-20
This is an exercise in cooperation and nonverbal communication.

Hunter and Hunted   Minutes: 20
When we can't see, our other senses really come into play.

Slow-Motion Fighting   Minutes: 20-30
Slow motion helps the coordination of the "fight" by giving performers a clear idea of when and where they should make their moves.

Lesson 10: Physicalization II

Emphasis: Controlling movement through the use of slow-motion activities.

Equipment: None

Hint: When "dying" in slow motion, be certain to practice safe falls with the entire group. Sometimes balance can be a problem, so stress that it is not necessary to do any "extreme" moves.

Slow-Motion Explosion Tag   Minutes: 20-30
Moving in slow motion takes a great deal of physical control. Falling in slow motion is a step-by-step process.

Slow-Motion Commentary   Minutes: 20
Following a partner's directions, whether verbal or nonverbal, can be an interesting beginning to ensemble work.

Mirror Game

DEMO
5
MINUTES

PLAYER PREP
0
MINUTES

PERFORMANCE
10+
MINUTES

Directions

- Players are divided into pairs: A and B.
- A is the movement initiator, B is the mirror.
- A starts a slow, simple movement and continues slowly.
- B mirrors A's movement exactly, always keeping eye contact.
- After a few minutes of silent mirroring, the director calls, "Switch!" and B takes over initiating the movement with A following.
- When the players switch, there should be no change in the ongoing moves.
- Play continues for another two or three minutes, as long as concentration continues.
- There should be no talking or giggling; students who find this difficult should be asked to observe.
- The total time for the mirroring should be fifteen to twenty minutes with switching and discussion.

Focus Questions

To the players:
- Was there a big difference when you were initiating rather than mirroring?
- Were there ever times when you could not tell if you were initiating or mirroring?
- Did the two of you generate a smooth rhythm?

To the observers:
- Could you tell who was A and who was B?
- Were there types of movements that worked better than others?
- Did keeping eye contact help?

This is an exercise in cooperation and nonverbal communication, not a game of fool the partner.

Type: Whole group
Skill: Beginning
Group Size: 2
Equipment: None

We play this game because:

Concentration with slow, smooth movement and unbroken eye contact can put players into a true ensemble.

Emphasis:

Blocking and Conventions

Characterization

Concentration

Creativity

Ensemble Acting

Following Directions

Give and Take Focus

Group Dynamics

Listening and Silence

Memorization

Nonverbal Communication

Observation

Physical Control

Plot Structure

Spontaneity

Storytelling

Hunter and Hunted

DEMO
0
MINUTES

PLAYER PREP
0
MINUTES

PERFORMANCE
10+
MINUTES

Type: Whole group
Skill: Beginning
Group Size: Whole group
Equipment: Blindfolds

We play this game because:
When we can't see, our other senses really come into play.

Emphasis:

Blocking and Conventions

Characterization

Concentration

Creativity

Ensemble Acting

Following Directions

Give and Take Focus

Group Dynamics

Listening and Silence

Memorization

Nonverbal Communication

Observation

Physical Control

Plot Structure

Spontaneity

Storytelling

Directions

- Players stand in a circle.
- Two players volunteer and go to the center. The rest of the players in the circle are now designated "spotters."
- Two more players are designated "spinners," and each takes one of the volunteers by the shoulder.
- Volunteers close their eyes or are blindfolded by the spinners.
- The spinners spin the volunteers around in the center of the circle, making sure they are far away from each other, then quietly return to their places in the circle.
- The blindfolded players are now designated "Hunter" and "Hunted."
- The Hunter tries to tag the Hunted. The Hunted tries to avoid being tagged.
- The spotters keep as quiet as possible to provide a quiet environment for the players.
- If the Hunter or Hunted gets too close to the perimeter, the spotters place them gently back in the center of the circle.
- When the Hunted is tagged, the spinners go to the middle to become the Hunter and Hunted and new spinners are chosen from the circle.

Focus Questions

- What technique did the Hunter use to find the Hunted? (Clothing noises, breathing, footsteps, etc.)
- What technique did the Hunted use to avoid the Hunter? (Clapping in one direction and moving in the other, crawling, etc.)
- How did the spotters contribute to the endeavor?
- What did it feel like not to be able to see?
- Which senses were heightened for the players?
- What distracted the players?

Avoid letting the spinners spin the players until they are dizzy.

Slow-Motion Fighting

DEMO
5
MINUTES

PLAYER PREP
0
MINUTES

PERFORMANCE
15+
MINUTES

Directions

- Two volunteers come to the front.
- When the director calls "Go!" the players begin to "fight" in slow motion. There may be *no* physical contact. Fighting may be in any style.
- The focus must be on the give and take. (When one player moves toward the other, the other must avoid her.)
- The "fight" is over after two to three minutes.

Focus Questions

- Was it difficult to give and take in slow motion?
- Was it difficult to avoid physical contact?
- Which movement technique worked the best (rolling, spinning, ducking, etc.)?
- Did the fight look like a dance?

Type: Improv
Skill: Beginning, Intermediate
Group Size: 2
Equipment: None

We play this game because:

Slow motion helps the coordination of the "fight" by giving performers a clear idea of when and where they should make their moves.

Emphasis:

Blocking and Conventions

Characterization

Concentration

Creativity

Ensemble Acting

Following Directions

Give and Take Focus

Group Dynamics

Listening and Silence

Memorization

Nonverbal Communication

Observation

Physical Control

Plot Structure

Spontaneity

Storytelling

Be aware of the temperament of your group! If they are an angry or rowdy bunch, exercise caution when or if you use this game. Don't hesitate to spend longer on demonstration and discussion.

Slow-Motion Explosion Tag

DEMO
5
MINUTES

PLAYER PREP
0
MINUTES

PERFORMANCE
15+
MINUTES

Type: Improv
Skill: Beginning
Group Size: 2
Equipment: None

We play this game because:

Moving in slow motion takes a great deal of physical control.

Emphasis:

Blocking and Conventions
Characterization
Concentration
Creativity
Ensemble Acting
Following Directions
Give and Take Focus
Group Dynamics
Listening and Silence
Memorization
Nonverbal Communication
Observation
Physical Control
Plot Structure
Spontaneity
Storytelling

Discuss

It's a good idea to demonstrate slow-motion exploding before you start the game. Have the whole group do it. Use these hints:
When falling, one should fall on one's side, from the ground up.
1. Start with the foot;
2. Roll onto the ankle;
3. Roll onto the side of the knee;
4. Followed by the thigh and hip;
5. Tuck the arm;
6. And roll onto the shoulder.
Avoid hitting kneecaps, wrists, and the head.

Directions

- The group stands in a large circle with five players in the middle.
- The five players start moving around in slow motion until they are told to freeze.
- The director chooses one of the players in the middle to be It.
- It must tag the other four players as they all move in slow motion in the middle of the circle.
- When tagged, the player must explode and fall to the ground in slow motion.

Focus Questions

- Was it difficult to move in slow motion?
- What kind of control did it take?
- What movement techniques did players use to try to avoid being tagged (pivots, spins, etc.)?
- What techniques did the person tagging use to get close to his victims in slow motion?
- Was there variety in explosions?
- How did the victims fall safely?

Slow-Motion Commentary

DEMO **0** MINUTES
PLAYER PREP **0** MINUTES
PERFORMANCE **20** MINUTES

Directions

- Two volunteers, A and B, come to the front of the group.
- A is the commentator/sportscaster. B is an athlete who performs a slow motion sport.
- B starts to move in slow motion, and A immediately starts the commentary on B's actions.
- B adapts to A's comments just as A adapts to B's movements.
- After a minute, A and B bring the scene to a natural ending.

Examples

Commentary:
- "Here we are at the annual pie-throwing event! Sam here has held the title for the last three years. And why? Well, look at his techniques! First he grasps the pie in his left hand ..."
- "Here we are at the final round of the ballet leaping event here as the Los Alamos County Fair. Susan here is competing for the title of Miss Leap Frog 2005! Rumor has it that she can leap over seven feet."

Athletic Events:
- Discus throwing.
- Auditions for the part of Billy Elliot.
- Auditions for the world's strangest walker.

Focus Questions

- Did the movement match the commentary?
- Did A follow B, or did B follow A?
- Could the audience tell who followed whom?
- Was it obvious to the audience that the improvisers knew who was the leader?
- From the point of view of A, did B understand what you were doing?
- From the point of view of B, did A lead you?

It is not so important that the movement is really clear — it may be suggested.

Type: Improv
Skill: Beginning/Intermediate
Group Size: 2
Equipment: None

We play this game because:

Following a partner's directions, whether verbal or nonverbal, can be an interesting beginning to ensemble work.

Emphasis:

Blocking and Conventions

Characterization

Concentration

Creativity

Ensemble Acting

Following Directions

Give and Take Focus

Group Dynamics

Listening and Silence

Memorization

Nonverbal Communication

Observation

Physical Control

Plot Structure

Spontaneity

Storytelling

Basic Acting and Group Skills

Lesson 11: Group Cohesion

Emphasis: Bonding through group work.

Equipment: Nametags, a ball, food (optional)

Hint: Not being — or allowing players to be — critical when players "mess up" is essential to creating an open and creative atmosphere for the rest of the semester.

Party Mix   Minutes: 10
Learning what others think of certain characters helps you focus on how to create characterizations.

It Wasn't My Fault   Minutes: 20
Players never seem to be at a loss for creative excuses, and this humorous activity breaks the ice!

Yes, And ...   Minutes: 20
Going with the flow is an important first step in improvisation and script writing.

Lesson 12: Nonverbal Acting

Emphasis: Beginning to act by creating characters and reacting to situations nonverbally.

Equipment: Chair or bench

Hint: Encourage the players to suggest situations for their entrances and/or exits, as this can create even more involvement. Stress that when reacting nonverbally, there is always a variety of movement.

Transformations   Minutes: 15-20
Moving from one end of an emotional and/or physical characterization to the other demonstrates the detail needed for broader characterization. (This game is known as "From ... to ..." in *Improv Ideas* page 160.)

Make an Entrance   Minutes: 25-40
Knowing and communicating stage areas and directions is critical to acting and improv. (This game is known as "Exit, Stage Right!" in *Improv Ideas* page 40.)

Party Mix

DEMO
0
MINUTES

PLAYER PREP
0
MINUTES

PERFORMANCE
5+
MINUTES

Directions

- Attach a nametag with a famous person's name to the back of each player as they enter the room.
- Players read the other players' names and react and interact with them as if they were that person.
- Players interact with others, although they do not know who they are supposed to be, always gleaning hints of their endowed identity from the other players.
- When players guess who they are they then "become" that famous person.

Focus Questions

- Which type of questions helped you guess your character?
- Were physical portrayals believable?

It helps if there are real party snacks and activities to make it as realistic as possible. (And it's fun!) Be sure you provide names of current celebrities that the group will recognize. You can find a helpful list in *Improv Ideas*:
Famous People — Page 59

Type: Whole group
Skill: Beginning
Group Size: Whole group
Equipment: Nametags, food and furniture if desired

We play this game because:

Learning what others think of certain characters helps you focus on how to create characterizations.

Emphasis:

Blocking and Conventions

Characterization

Concentration

Creativity

Ensemble Acting

Following Directions

Give and Take Focus

Group Dynamics

Listening and Silence

Memorization

Nonverbal Communication

Observation

Physical Control

Plot Structure

Spontaneity

Storytelling

It Wasn't My Fault

DEMO
0
MINUTES

PLAYER PREP
0
MINUTES

PERFORMANCE
15+
MINUTES

Type: Whole group
Skill: Beginning
Group Size: Whole group
Equipment: None

We play this game because:

Players never seem to be at a loss for creative excuses, and this humorous activity breaks the ice!

Emphasis:

Blocking and Conventions

Characterization

Concentration

Creativity

Ensemble Acting

Following Directions

Give and Take Focus

Group Dynamics

Listening and Silence

Memorization

Nonverbal Communication

Observation

Physical Control

Plot Structure

Spontaneity

Storytelling

Directions

- Players line up in two lines on each side of the playing area, facing each other.
- One at a time a player from one side then the other side takes Center Stage and gives an excuse for being late to class or not having homework.
- When players give an excuse, they go to the end of their original line.
- The pace should be fast.

Focus Questions

- Was it difficult to think that quickly in the allotted time?
- Did you feel comfortable just saying the first thing that came to mind?
- Were there creative responses?
- Did the excuses get more or less creative the longer the game was played?

Discuss actual excuses players use or have used in school *after* this exercise. (A sneaky director might add this to a master list for future use.) You can find a helpful list in *Improv Ideas*:
Excuses — Page 45

Yes, And ...

DEMO	PLAYER PREP	PERFORMANCE
0	**0**	**3+**
MINUTES	MINUTES	MINUTES

Directions

- The group spreads out around the room.
- One player calls out an activity. ("Let's go to the beach!")
- All players then move as if they are on the beach.
- Another player adds to this activity with a "Yes, and" response. ("Yes, and let's build a sand castle.")
- Players engage in this activity.
- Another player adds more. ("Yes, and let's make it really huge!")
- The play continues for about 3-5 minutes.
- A new scene starts.

Focus Questions

- Was it difficult to add group activities?
- Was it difficult to join in the activity?
- Was it difficult to flow into the next activity?
- Was it important to be silent, or did talking help?

Yes, And ... can also be played in pairs. A new variation from the folks at the Loose Moose in Canada is to allow a "no" response, but one that is said in a positive way that bridges into a new, more acceptable activity.

Type: Whole group
Skill: Beginning/Intermediate
Group Size: Whole group
Equipment: Clear room of obstacles

We play this game because:

Going with the flow is an important first step in improvisation and script writing.

Emphasis:

Blocking and Conventions
Characterization
Concentration
Creativity
Ensemble Acting
Following Directions
Give and Take Focus
Group Dynamics
Listening and Silence
Memorization
Nonverbal Communication
Observation
Physical Control
Plot Structure
Spontaneity
Storytelling

Transformations

DEMO 3 MINUTES **PLAYER PREP 0 MINUTES** **PERFORMANCE 5+ MINUTES**

Type: Improv
Skill: Beginning/Intermediate
Group Size: 1
Equipment: None

We play this game because:

Moving from one end of an emotional or physical characterization to the other demonstrates the detail needed for broader characterization.

Emphasis:

Blocking and Conventions
Characterization
Concentration
Creativity
Ensemble Acting
Following Directions
Give and Take Focus
Group Dynamics
Listening and Silence
Memorization
Nonverbal Communication
Observation
Physical Control
Plot Structure
Spontaneity
Storytelling

Directions

- Players line up on one side of the playing area.
- The director calls out a transformation as the first player progresses from one side of the playing area to the other.
- The player makes the transformation gradually during the cross. The player may speak and create imaginary props or players as needed.
- The director may change the transformation for each player or continue with the same one to see individual variations on a theme.

Examples

- From criminal to victim: Player runs on laughing wildly. He looks around, tiptoes to the center of the playing area, looks around again, looks terrified, puts his hands up, and walks backward off the stage as a holdup victim.
- From stoic to hysterical: Player enters walking slowly and upright, nothing bothering her. When she hits Center, she gazes out as if confused. She turns to go, looks again, and runs off in hysterics, having seen the full extent of the devastation.

Focus Questions

- Did the players show how the transformations were motivated?
- Did the players use variety in their actions?
- Did the players make use of pauses?
- Were the changes gradual?

Discuss films in which transformations exist: *Dr. Jekyll and Mr. Hyde, The Picture of Dorian Grey,* etc. You can find a helpful list in *Improv Ideas*: Transformations — Page 161

Make an Entrance

DEMO **10** MINUTES   **PLAYER PREP** **0** MINUTES   **PERFORMANCE** **15+** MINUTES

Discuss

- Stage areas and directions. Players should always note where the audience is on their stage maps.
- Stress the importance of motivating the movement.

Directions

- Distribute stage area maps (see *Appendix*, page 212).
- One player at a time is chosen to enter the playing area and cross to Center.
- The player is given an entrance *as if* and an area from which to enter.
- The player enters as directed.
- After the player has entered and crossed to the chair or bench, the director gives an exit *as if* and an area through which to exit.
- The player exits as directed.

Examples

- Enter from Down Right. Cross to Center as if you are about to hear bad news. Exit Up Right as if you have heard good news.
- Starting at Down Left, exit Up Left as if you are going to hide.

Focus Questions

- What tricks do you use to remember Stage Right and Left? Upstage and Downstage?
- Is it more difficult using stage directions when you are actually on-stage or when you're just talking about it?

Scenes don't have to go together, but it helps if the entrance and exit are logical, especially for beginners.

Type: Whole group
Skill: Beginning/Intermediate
Group Size: 1
Equipment: Chair or bench

We play this game because:
Knowing and communicating stage areas and directions is critical to acting and improv.

Emphasis:

Blocking and Conventions
Characterization
Concentration
Creativity
Ensemble Acting
Following Directions
Give and Take Focus
Group Dynamics
Listening and Silence
Memorization
Nonverbal Communication
Observation
Physical Control
Plot Structure
Spontaneity
Storytelling

What Is It? Observing and Working Together

Lesson 13: Ensemble Acting

Emphasis: Combining sound and movement to create a cohesive whole.

Equipment: None

Hint: Although sound and movement are coordinated in a mechanical manner, machines do not need to be working and recognizable. Avoid assembly lines!

The Machine Game	**Minutes: 20-30**

Working together as an ensemble takes much coordination and creativity.

The Metaphor Machine   **Minutes: 30**

Aspects of a theme can work together to create a whole.

Lesson 14: Observation

Emphasis: Observing our environment — a basic skill in acting.

Equipment: Generic objects, a stick, covered tray, chalkboard, index cards, pencils

Hint: Start your next session by asking players if they noticed any new things as a result of playing these games!

Pass the Object   **Minutes: 10**

We use our entire bodies to react to creative stimuli.

Pass the Stick   **Minutes: 10**

Our imaginations can stretch so that an ordinary object can become much more than it appears.

Objects on a Tray   **Minutes: 20**

Observing the little things around us and the details about them can make us more aware.

Change Three Things   **Minutes: 20**

Observing small details is essential to creating a character.

The Machine Game

DEMO
5+
MINUTES

PLAYER PREP
5+
MINUTES

PERFORMANCE
3
MINUTES

Directions

- The director chooses five to seven volunteers.
- One player starts a simple sound and movement.
- Another player adds to this sound/movement as if part of a mechanical machine.
- The next player adds another sound and movement to go with the first two.
- Play continues until all players are working their sounds and movements in harmony.
- Director calls out "Faster" and "Slower" to see if the machine is really working as a unit.
- Note: the players do not have to form a recognizable machine.

Focus Questions

- What movements seemed to coordinate with others?
- How could you tell if the movement was working together?
- What kinds of movement didn't work?
- How did the group get the machine to function as a whole?
- Did the sounds fit the mechanical movements?
- Could the machine function well and together as they went faster and slower?

Type: Improv
Skill: Beginning
Group Size: 5-7
Equipment: None

We play this game because:
Working together as an ensemble takes much coordination.

Emphasis:

Blocking and Conventions
Characterization
Concentration
Creativity
Ensemble Acting
Following Directions
Give and Take Focus
Group Dynamics
Listening and Silence
Memorization
Nonverbal Communication
Observation
Physical Control
Plot Structure
Spontaneity
Storytelling

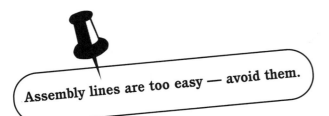

Assembly lines are too easy — avoid them.

The Metaphor Machine

DEMO
5
MINUTES

PLAYER PREP
10
MINUTES

PERFORMANCE
3+
MINUTES

Type: Whole group
Skill: Beginning/Intermediate
Group Size: 5-7
Equipment: None

We play this game because:

Aspects of a theme can work together to create a whole.

Emphasis:

Blocking and Conventions
Characterization
Concentration
Creativity
Ensemble Acting
Following Directions
Give and Take Focus
Group Dynamics
Listening and Silence
Memorization
Nonverbal Communication
Observation
Physical Control
Plot Structure
Spontaneity
Storytelling

Directions

- Divide into groups of five to seven players.
- Give each group a type of machine to create.
- Each group gets three to five minutes to create a machine using synchronized sound and movement. The sound is a word or phrase that helps create the type of machine.

Examples

Possible Machines
- The School Spirit Machine
- The Halloween Machine
- The MTV Machine
- The Lunchroom Machine
- The Horror Movie Machine

"Homework Machine" components could include: "Do your Homework." "Leave me alone!" "This is too hard!" "Where is my pencil?" "I need Help!" "It's time for *Friends*." "I don't want to." "Can you come over?" "I'm going to flunk!" in synchronized movement.

Focus Questions

- Was it difficult to find aspects of the topic in sounds/phrases?
- How did you coordinate the words to the movement?
- Did the parts of the machine work together?

Thinking metaphorically can be difficult for some players. Discuss "aspects of" or "parts of" to clarify.

Pass the Object

Directions

- Players stand or sit in a circle.
- The director chooses a neutral object such as a ruler, a volleyball, or a teddy bear to pass around the circle clockwise.
- As the object is quickly passed and received, the director calls out an attribute to which the players passing and receiving must respond. These may be called every four or five passes to keep the passing going and observe variety.
- The director may wish to use a checklist to keep track of attributes used.
- The object should be passed around the circle at least three times.

Examples

- It's hot!
- It's fragile!
- It's heavy!
- It's illegal!
- It's stinky!

Focus Questions

- Was it difficult to switch reactions?
- Did the rate of passing help the interpretation of reactions, or did it need to be slowed down or sped up?
- Did you use your whole body to react, or did you just use your facial expressions?

You can find a helpful list in *Improv Ideas*: Attributes — Page 19

Type: Whole group
Skill: Beginning
Group Size: Whole group
Equipment: Generic objects

We play this game because:
We use our entire bodies to react to creative stimuli.

Emphasis:

Blocking and Conventions
Characterization
Concentration
Creativity
Ensemble Acting
Following Directions
Give and Take Focus
Group Dynamics
Listening and Silence
Memorization
Nonverbal Communication
Observation
Physical Control
Plot Structure
Spontaneity
Storytelling

Pass the Stick

DEMO
0
MINUTES

PLAYER PREP
0
MINUTES

PERFORMANCE
5+
MINUTES

Type: Whole group
Skill: Beginning
Group Size: Whole group
Equipment: A stick

We play this game because:

Our imaginations can stretch so that an ordinary object can become much more than it appears.

Emphasis:

Blocking and Conventions

Characterization

Concentration

Creativity

Ensemble Acting

Following Directions

Give and Take Focus

Group Dynamics

Listening and Silence

Memorization

Nonverbal Communication

Observation

Physical Control

Plot Structure

Spontaneity

Storytelling

Directions

- Players stand or sit in a circle.
- Player one passes a stick to the player on his left.
- The stick must be used as a different object each time it is passed.
- The stick should go around the circle at least twice.
- Do not allow players to pass.

Examples

- Player one uses the stick as a whip.
- Player two uses the stick as a microphone.
- Player three uses the stick as a snake.
- Player four uses the stick as an eyelash curler.
- Player five uses the stick as a baby.

Focus Questions

- Was it difficult to think of a use for the stick?
- Were the uses limited by the shape? If not, how did the player suggest another shape?
- Did you have to involve your whole body while acting the usage?
- What body parts were used the most often?
- Was it often necessary to use words or sounds?

Objects on a Tray

DEMO
0
MINUTES

PLAYER PREP
0
MINUTES

PERFORMANCE
15+
MINUTES

Directions

- Players sit facing one direction.
- The director places a covered tray in front of all the players and lifts the cover to reveal fifteen to twenty-five small objects. (Objects may include such easily recognized things as a stapler, a rubber band, a cassette tape, a ribbon, a straw, etc.)
- The players get three minutes to view the objects before the tray is re-covered. They may walk around the tray, but may not touch the tray or its contents.
- After the tray is re-covered, the players have three minutes to write down as many objects as they can remember.
- The director asks, "How many thought there were fifteen objects?" "Sixteen?" "Seventeen?" etc., and tallies the votes for each number.
- A player reads her list as the director writes it on the chalkboard.
- The group adds to the list until all objects are identified.

Focus Questions

- Which objects were remembered the most frequently? Why?
- Which objects were most often forgotten?
- Do you think that shape, color, or familiarity had anything to do with this?
- What did you learn about your own powers of observation from this exercise?
- What would you do differently in the future?
- What strategies did different people use to try to remember the objects?

Type: Whole group
Skill: Beginning
Group Size: Whole group
Equipment: Covered tray, generic objects, chalkboard, index cards, pencils

We play this game because:

Observing the little things around us and the details about them can make us more aware.

Emphasis:

Blocking and Conventions

Characterization

Concentration

Creativity

Ensemble Acting

Following Directions

Give and Take Focus

Group Dynamics

Listening and Silence

Memorization

Nonverbal Communication

Observation

Physical Control

Plot Structure

Spontaneity

Storytelling

Change Three Things

DEMO
0
MINUTES

PLAYER PREP
0
MINUTES

PERFORMANCE
15+
MINUTES

Type: Whole group
Skill: Beginning
Group Size: Whole group
Equipment: None

We play this game because:

Observing small details is essential in creating a character.

Emphasis:

Blocking and Conventions

Characterization

Concentration

Creativity

Ensemble Acting

Following Directions

Give and Take Focus

Group Dynamics

Listening and Silence

Memorization

Nonverbal Communication

Observation

Physical Control

Plot Structure

Spontaneity

Storytelling

Directions

- Five players sit in various positions in a row of chairs across the front of the room.
- The director calls "Freeze."
- The rest of the group takes a mental photograph of the five seated players.
- The group turns their backs for two minutes while the seated players change three things about themselves (leg crossed the other way, sleeve rolled up, shoe untied, etc).
- The group turns back around and volunteers try to identify the three things each seated player changed.
- If they guess all three, they may take that player's place in front of the group.
- The game resumes with five new players.

Focus Questions

- What changes were the easiest/hardest to guess?
- How did you manage to remember the mental picture?
- What changes seemed most creative to you?

Stress that the changes should not be so subtle that they can't be guessed fairly easily.

Hold It Right There

Lesson 15: Frozen Pictures I

Emphasis: Beginning awareness of stage pictures.

Equipment: Stools, benches, chairs

Hint: The students love to play photographer! Don't forget to bring in your own family portraits to share.

Family Portraits   Minutes: 60

The family portrait is usually a student's first experience in stage groupings.

Lesson 16: Frozen Pictures II

Emphasis: Using prompts and focus in frozen pictures.

Equipment: Chairs, benches, selected props

Hint: Stills from films are very valuable for emotional freezes. Introducing the concept of focus in simple frozen pictures stretches the imagination and is just plain fun!

Emotional Freezes   Minutes: 30

Frozen pictures can express an emotion, or individual performers can express aspects of that emotion.

Props Freeze   Minutes: 30

Focusing on an object provides a stimulus for the tableau.

Hold It Right There (Continued)

Lesson 17: More Frozen Pictures

Emphasis: How situations and focus create interesting variety in frozen stage pictures.

Equipment: Chairs, benches

Hint: Just for fun, call out names to give and take focus.

Movie Theatre   Minutes: 60

Focusing on characters' reactions to other characters in the scene shows how there may be a variety of ways to express one focus.

Lesson 18: Movement Freezes

Emphasis: Prompts motivating interesting stage pictures to be brought to life in improv scenes.

Equipment: Chairs, benches, levels

Hint: It is very important to stress that the pictures don't really have to make sense. As the players become more familiar with working together quickly, the images will become more interesting and varied. For added fun, bring a few to life!

Yearbook Game   Minutes: 30

The topic can inspire individuals to interact as an ensemble.

Freeze Titles   Minutes: 25

Levels help create interesting stage pictures.

Family Portraits

DEMO
5
MINUTES

PLAYER PREP
10
MINUTES

PERFORMANCE
5
MINUTES

Discuss

What makes an interesting group photograph/portrait? (Levels, spacing, body position, facial expression, relationships, gestures, etc.)

Directions

- Divide into groups of five.
- Each player decides what his or her position is in the family.
- Groups arrange three types of family portraits: the perfect one that hangs over the mantle, the one with one flaw, and the one in which many things go wrong.
- All groups show their portraits to the entire group.

Examples

- A family with a father, mother, twin girls, and a baby brother.
- A family with a father, mother, son, daughter, and dog.
- A family with a single parent and four children

Focus Questions

- Were the groupings interesting to observe in terms of visual variety?
- Was it easy to determine each player's position/age/status in the family?
- Were relationships clearly communicated? How?
- What "flaws" were explored?

Type: Prepared
Skill: Beginning
Group Size: 5
Equipment: Chairs, stools, benches

We play this game because:

Most players will remember having sat for a family portrait and how carefully the photographer arranged the family members.

Emphasis:

Blocking and Conventions
Characterization
Concentration
Creativity
Ensemble Acting
Following Directions
Give and Take Focus
Group Dynamics
Listening and Silence
Memorization
Nonverbal Communication
Observation
Physical Control
Plot Structure
Spontaneity
Storytelling

Emotional Freezes

DEMO
0
MINUTES

PLAYER PREP
10
MINUTES

PERFORMANCE
3
MINUTES

Type: Prepared
Skill: Beginning
Group Size: 3-5
Equipment: Chairs, benches, props

We play this game because:

Frozen pictures can express an emotion, or individual performers can express aspects of that emotion.

Emphasis:

Blocking and Conventions

Characterization

Concentration

Creativity

Ensemble Acting

Following Directions

Give and Take Focus

Group Dynamics

Listening and Silence

Memorization

Nonverbal Communication

Observation

Physical Control

Plot Structure

Spontaneity

Storytelling

Directions

- Divide into groups of three to five players.
- Assign all groups the same three emotions.
- Each group makes three separate frozen pictures in which the overall emotional feeling is shown.

Examples

- Joy: A family welcomes mother and new baby home from the hospital.
- Anger: Two students fight over a referee call in a soccer game.
- Sadness: A group of students finds an injured dog on the school playground.

Focus Questions

- Did each new freeze convey an overall emotion?
- Was each freeze interesting to observe? Did it use levels, spacing, facial expressions, etc.?
- Was each character in the scene clearly defined?
- How did the different groups interpret the emotions differently?
- Was there a specific focus?

Discuss how one emotion may be expressed in many different ways.

Props Freeze

DEMO
5
MINUTES

PLAYER PREP
3
MINUTES

PERFORMANCE
3
MINUTES

Directions

- Players divide into groups of five.
- Director gives each group one prop.
- The groups have three minutes to plan three different frozen pictures using the prop as a different object in each.

Examples

- A floppy hat may be a dead animal, a present, or a new baby.
- A cell phone could be a candy bar, an object of worship, or a bomb.

Focus Questions

- Was it clear what the prop was supposed to be?
- Was the prop the focus of the freeze?
- Did the freeze show action?
- Did the freeze effectively use variety (gestures, body position, facial expression, levels, etc.)?

Type: Prepared
Skill: Beginning
Group Size: 5
Equipment: Props

We play this game because:
Focusing on an object provides a stimulus for the tableau.

Emphasis:

Blocking and Conventions
Characterization
Concentration
Creativity
Ensemble Acting
Following Directions
Give and Take Focus
Group Dynamics
Listening and Silence
Memorization
Nonverbal Communication
Observation
Physical Control
Plot Structure
Spontaneity
Storytelling

Try to find props that are not so specific that they couldn't suggest something else by shape, color, size, etc.

Movie Theatre

DEMO
0
MINUTES

PLAYER PREP
10
MINUTES

PERFORMANCE
5
MINUTES

Type: Prepared
Skill: Intermediate
Group Size: 5-7
Equipment: Chairs and benches

We play this game because:

Focusing on characters' reactions to other characters in the scene shows how there may be a variety of ways to express focus.

Emphasis:

Blocking and Conventions

Characterization

Concentration

Creativity

Ensemble Acting

Following Directions

Give and Take Focus

Group Dynamics

Listening and Silence

Memorization

Nonverbal Communication

Observation

Physical Control

Plot Structure

Spontaneity

Storytelling

Directions

- Players divide into groups of five to seven.
- Each group gets chairs or benches to make two rows of an imaginary movie theatre.
- Each group decides on a specific film or type of film to view.
- In a sequence of ten short frozen pictures, the group develops a five-minute "story" that shows the group's reaction to the film and one another from the moment they enter the theatre to the time they exit.

Examples

- A group of high school friends gathers excitedly to see the latest gruesome horror film. It turns out to be too gruesome.
- Three couples who don't know each other come to see the latest romantic comedy. Since the lead male dies in the middle, the film is not so romantic after all.

Focus Questions

- How did the characters show their interactions?
- Was the environment used?
- How was the genre of the film shown?
- Did the story have a beginning, a middle, and an ending?

Bring the scene to life! Use this as a "take focus" exercise.

Yearbook Game

| DEMO
0
MINUTES | PLAYER PREP
1
MINUTES | PERFORMANCE
20+
MINUTES |

Directions

- Divide into teams of five.
- Players think of, draw, or are assigned the name of a real or fictitious school club and are asked to form a frozen picture (tableau) that expresses the characteristics of the club.
- They have one minute to prepare the picture.
- Groups perform for one another.

Focus Questions

- Did the players use different levels, facial expressions, body positions, spacing, and gestures?
- Did the pictures create an interesting interpretation on the idea of the club?
- Did the pictures hold together as a unit, or was it mainly just individuals?
- Was the picture visually interesting? Why?
- Did the picture tell a story of any kind?

Challenge Players to Ramp It Up!

- Create frozen pictures of the same clubs ten or twenty years in the future.
- Bring the pictures to life.

Show pictures in an actual yearbook and discuss how they express the personality of the activity.

Type: Improv
Skill: Beginning
Group Size: 5
Equipment: Levels

We play this game because:
The topic can inspire individuals to interact as an ensemble.

Emphasis:

Blocking and Conventions
Characterization
Concentration
Creativity
Ensemble Acting
Following Directions
Give and Take Focus
Group Dynamics
Listening and Silence
Memorization
Nonverbal Communication
Observation
Physical Control
Plot Structure
Spontaneity
Storytelling

Freeze Titles

DEMO — **2** MINUTES

PLAYER PREP — **0** MINUTES

PERFORMANCE — **5+** MINUTES

Type: Improv
Skill: Beginning
Group Size: 5
Equipment: Chairs, benches

We play this game because:

Subtle physical changes can throw a completely new slant on similar situations.

Emphasis:

Blocking and Conventions

Characterization

Concentration

Creativity

Ensemble Acting

Following Directions

Give and Take Focus

Group Dynamics

Listening and Silence

Memorization

Nonverbal Communication

Observation

Physical Control

Plot Structure

Spontaneity

Storytelling

Directions

- Director chooses five players to come to the front of the group and move around randomly using the various levels while the director counts slowly to ten.
- On the count of ten, the director calls out "Freeze!"
- The players take one second to create a picture from their positions.
- Volunteers from the class call out titles for the pictures ("Our Family Vacation," "Prom," "Disney World," "The Beach," "Trapped in the Darkness," "Joe Sleeps In," "Surfing Isn't Fun," "The Dog Who Ate Our Lunch," etc.)
- The same volunteers move again to the count of ten and the play continues.

Focus Questions

- Was it difficult to group into a picture so quickly?
- Did the levels help make interesting pictures?
- Did the pictures go together? Why or why not?
- Were there characters in the pictures?
- Were the titles creative/suitable?

It really doesn't matter if the titles make sense! Players will get more creative with practice. Levels help create interesting stage pictures.

Freeze Frame

Lesson 19: A Story in Frozen Pictures

Emphasis: Continuing with frozen pictures, this time telling a historical story in frozen pictures.

Equipment: Assorted levels

Hint: Before starting, sit in a circle and discuss visits players may have had to different wax museums. Focus on wax scenes (not single figures) that made an impression.

Wax Museum   Minutes: 50-60

Well-known historical situations can provide a variety of frozen pictures, from chronological narratives to point-of-view scenes focusing on individuals' reactions to the situation.

Lesson 20: Stories in Frozen Pictures

May take 2 class periods

Emphasis: Telling an original story in frozen pictures concentrating on the plot structure of a beginning, a middle, and an ending.

Equipment: Chairs, benches, stools

Hint: Give players as much time as they seem to need. Emphasize that some of the players will need to show exaggerated movement.

The Accident   Minutes: 60+

Frozen pictures can tell a story without movement or sound. In this game, the focus is on plot.

Wax Museum

DEMO
0
MINUTES

PLAYER PREP
10
MINUTES

PERFORMANCE
3+
MINUTES

Type: Prepared
Skill: Intermediate
Group Size: 5-7
Equipment: Assorted levels

We play this game because:

This is an entertaining way of combining stage picture awareness and chronological plot development.

Emphasis:

Blocking and Conventions
Characterization
Concentration
Creativity
Ensemble Acting
Following Directions
Give and Take Focus
Group Dynamics
Listening and Silence
Memorization
Nonverbal Communication
Observation
Physical Control
Plot Structure
Spontaneity
Storytelling

Directions

- Divide into groups of four to six.
- Each group thinks of, draws, or is assigned a historical moment.
- Groups develop three to five "pictures" representing aspects of that moment.
- When finished, groups perform for each other. Frozen scenes should be performed in chronological order. Historical accuracy is not required!

Examples

King Tut's Tomb Opened
1. Workers dig furiously while Carter looks up with anxiety.
2. One worker turns to Carter with a look of triumph as the others dig with their hands.
3. Everyone stands back in awe as a huge door is revealed.
4. The door is gingerly pulled open.
5. Carter enters and gasps in amazement as the others crowd around outside the door asking, "Do you see anything?"

Focus Questions

- Was each picture heightened by a particularly emotional moment?
- Were the moments cumulative in intensity?
- Did the moments contain a story with a beginning, a middle, and an ending?
- Were the pictures visually interesting and varied?

If your students do not know much about the historical moment, let them imagine what it might have been!
You can find a helpful list in *Improv Ideas*: Historical Moments — Page 87

The Accident

Discuss

Types of accidents (tripping, spilled water, a car accident, being hit by a baseball, etc.).

Directions

- The group is divided into groups of four or five.
- Each group decides on what type of accident they will portray in five frozen pictures.
- Each freeze must illustrate the story of the accident in chronological order from its beginning to its conclusion.
- Each scene should contain as much frozen action as possible.

Examples

The Water Spill
1. The scene is the school hallway before school. Two students are at their lockers. Two other students are just coming down the hall.
2. One of the locker students is at the drinking fountain where it flows over and soaks her clothes. Her friend is still at the locker, laughing. The others have reached the scene and don't notice because …
3. … the locker students are proceeding down the hall as one of the others slips in the water and begins to fall. Her friend tries to catch her.
4. The fallen girl is lying on the ground in a twisted position as her friend, at her side, calls for help. The other two turn around.
5. Three girls are crowded around the fallen girl as they try to help her up.

Focus Questions

- Did each picture follow the one preceding it logically?
- Did each picture tell a story?
- Were the characters clear?
- Did the pictures have a focus?
- Did the pictures show action?

Type: Prepared
Skill: Beginning/Intermediate
Group Size: 4-5
Equipment: None

We play this game because:

Frozen pictures can tell a story without movement or sound. In this game, the focus is on plot.

Emphasis:

Blocking and Conventions
Characterization
Concentration
Creativity
Ensemble Acting
Following Directions
Give and Take Focus
Group Dynamics
Listening and Silence
Memorization
Nonverbal Communication
Observation
Physical Control
Plot Structure
Spontaneity
Storytelling

Look This Way

Lesson 21: Give and Take Focus I

Emphasis: Being aware of when to give and take focus in scenes.

Equipment: Benches, chairs

Hint: Being the center of attention is a concept students can relate to! All they need to do is to apply the knowledge they learned in Units 9 and 10!

Take Focus   Minutes: 20

Finding physical ways to take the focus in a scene is a necessary skill in acting. Conversely, when one has the focus, others on-stage need to support him/her by giving focus.

School Bus   Minutes: 30

Moving from freezes into action and back into freezes is a good way to reinforce the concept of focus.

Lesson 22: Give and Take Focus II

Emphasis: Sharing focus in a scene.

Equipment: Chairs (optional)

Hint: Since so many students have cell phones these days, you may have to remind them what a phone bank is (or was)! You may also find that they prefer to use their cell phones as props in this exercise.

Phone Booth   Minutes: 50-60

Giving and taking focus is essential when performing any scene with more than one actor.

Take Focus

DEMO
3
MINUTES

PLAYER PREP
0
MINUTES

PERFORMANCE
3+
MINUTES

Directions

- Five players sit on one or two benches and assume neutral frozen positions.
- The director chooses a generic situation.
- On the count of three, all players react to the situation. Then one player is singled out to "take focus."
- The rest of the players immediately adjust their positions to give the singled-out player the focus, and the freeze resumes.
- A new situation is called out with another player taking the focus.

Examples

- Spectators at a baseball game
- Guests at a surprise party
- Friends on a roller coaster
- Dancers in a chorus line
- Passengers on an airplane in turbulence

Focus Questions

- Did the original freeze have a focus? If so, how and why?
- Was the focused freeze more interesting?
- Did the focused freeze tell a more specific story?

Try playing this with really exaggerated types of focus for a start. For example, when one takes focus we must *not* remain in the same position (seated, full front, etc.).

Type: Improv
Skill: Beginning
Group Size: 5
Equipment: Benches

We play this game because:

Knowing how to give and take focus without losing our characterization is a crucial acting skill.

Emphasis:

Blocking and Conventions
Characterization
Concentration
Creativity
Ensemble Acting
Following Directions
Give and Take Focus
Group Dynamics
Listening and Silence
Memorization
Nonverbal Communication
Observation
Physical Control
Plot Structure
Spontaneity
Storytelling

School Bus

DEMO
0
MINUTES

PLAYER PREP
0
MINUTES

PERFORMANCE
10
MINUTES

Type: Improv
Skill: Beginning/Intermediate
Group Size: 9
Equipment: Chairs

We play this game because:

Moving from freezes into action and back into freezes is a good way to reinforce the concept of focus.

Emphasis:

Blocking and Conventions

Characterization

Concentration

Creativity

Ensemble Acting

Following Directions

Give and Take Focus

Group Dynamics

Listening and Silence

Memorization

Nonverbal Communication

Observation

Physical Control

Plot Structure

Spontaneity

Storytelling

Directions

- Choose nine players. Eight will be the passengers on the school bus; one will be the driver.
- Players sit in chairs arranged as if on a bus.
- Each player silently creates a character.
- On the director's count of three, the passengers and driver freeze in character.
- When the director calls "Unfreeze," the scene briefly comes to life until the director calls "Freeze" again.
- Audience members determine whether or not there is a focus.
- If there is no focus, the director will call for a specific player to take focus in the next freeze.
- The game continues as before.

Examples

- Most of the students on the bus are well behaved, but one particular student tries to bully another.
- The driver is extremely nervous and keeps trying to discipline students while driving.

Focus Questions

- Did the original freeze have a focus?
- Did focus emerge when the scene was unfrozen? Why or why not?
- Was the scene more interesting when a particular focus was decided?

Phone Booth

DEMO
0
MINUTES

PLAYER PREP
0
MINUTES

PERFORMANCE
10+
MINUTES

Discuss

- Director chooses five volunteers to come to the front of the group.
- Players are assigned a number (1-5) and stand in a line with their backs to the audience.
- As each number is called, the player with that number turns around to face the audience and starts a telephone conversation.
- When the next player's number is called, the previous speaker turns her back to the audience but continues the conversation, only softer.
- The player whose number was called starts a conversation, another number is called, and the game continues until all numbers have been called several times.
- When a player's number is called for the second or third time, she faces the audience and continues her conversation in the original, louder tone.
- At the director's signal, all players turn to face the audience and continue to speak all at once.
- The director then calls each number, and the game continues by giving and taking focus, with all players facing the audience.

Examples

- One talks about a test he just took.
- Two passes on a juicy piece of gossip.
- Three tries to persuade someone to go to a party.
- Four tries to order clothing.
- Five tries to borrow money from a parent.

Focus Questions

- Was it difficult to continue a conversation while someone else had the focus?
- Was it difficult to continue where you left off when you had the focus?
- Could you continue your conversation while others around you were talking?
- Were the conversations involving?

Type: Improv
Skill: Beginning/Intermediate
Group Size: 5
Equipment: None

We play this game because:

Giving and taking focus is essential when performing any scene with more than one actor.

Emphasis:

Blocking and Conventions
Characterization
Concentration
Creativity
Ensemble Acting
Following Directions
Give and Take Focus
Group Dynamics
Listening and Silence
Memorization
Nonverbal Communication
Observation
Physical Control
Plot Structure
Spontaneity
Storytelling

Natural and Unplanned — Spontaneity

Lesson 23: Spontaneity I

Emphasis: Starting improvisation by playing basic games which stress spontaneity and accepting offers.

Equipment: Two chairs or one bench

Hint: Students love to die dramatically. This keeps the fun and pace going as well as making "losing" fun. It is very important to emphasize that there is not any winning or losing.

Change It!   Minutes: 15
Using body positions as prompts for a simple scene is an important beginning improv skill.

Gimme That Seat   Minutes: 10
Giving and accepting offers is the first step in creating improvisations. Go with what is offered.

Story, Story, Die   Minutes: 20
By having to concentrate intensely on what is being said, we develop better concentration, observation, and creativity.

Lesson 24: Spontaneity II

Emphasis: Concentrating on keeping up a fast pace in order to keep the ideas flowing with basic games.

Equipment: Category ideas

Hint: All these games can be used as warm-ups in any day's lesson plan as their spontaneity value and interest levels are high!

Line at a Time   Minutes: 10-15
A great warm-up and ice breaker that encourages creativity and non-judgmental performance. (Just do it!)

Tell Me About the Time You … (TMATTY)   Minutes: 15-20
This is a great warm-up and a speed game that encourages quick thinking under time constraints.

Word Tennis   Minutes: 15-20
Listening and thinking quickly on your feet are essential improvisation and acting skills.

Change It!

DEMO	PLAYER PREP	PERFORMANCE
5 MINUTES	**0** MINUTES	**10** MINUTES

Directions

- The entire group stands in a circle.
- One player enters the center of the circle and moves around until the director calls "Freeze."
- The first player holds the freeze as another volunteer enters the center and starts a scene based on player one's body position.
- Player one unfreezes and plays a very brief (30-second) scene with player two.
- Player one finds a motivation to exit.
- Player two freezes as another player enters the circle and a new scene begins.

Focus Questions

- Were the frozen body positions used to suggest the scenes?
- Did the frozen player take the offer and continue the suggested scene or did he try to adapt it?
- Was the scene understandable?
- Were the exits motivated?
- Did the scenes proceed rapidly without lag time?

Type: Whole group
Skill: Beginning/intermediate
Group Size: Whole group
Equipment: None

We play this game because:

Using body positions as prompts for a simple scene is an important beginning improv skill.

Emphasis:

Blocking and Conventions
Characterization
Concentration
Creativity
Ensemble Acting
Following Directions
Give and Take Focus
Group Dynamics
Listening and Silence
Memorization
Nonverbal Communication
Observation
Physical Control
Plot Structure
Spontaneity
Storytelling

Gimme That Seat

DEMO
0
MINUTES

PLAYER PREP
0
MINUTES

PERFORMANCE
10
MINUTES

Type: Improv
Skill: Beginning
Group Size: 5-10
Equipment: Chairs and/or benches

We play this game because:
Giving and accepting offers is the first step in creating improvisations. Go with what is offered.

Emphasis:

Blocking and Conventions

Characterization

Concentration

Creativity

Ensemble Acting

Following Directions

Give and Take Focus

Group Dynamics

Listening and Silence

Memorization

Nonverbal Communication

Observation

Physical Control

Plot Structure

Spontaneity

Storytelling

Directions

- The director places a chair in front of the group.
- Five to ten players line up at the right side of the chair.
- The first player sits on the chair.
- The next player in line comes up to the seated player and makes him an offer to get him out of the chair (see examples).
- The seated player must leave, motivated by the other player's reason.
- The second player sits in the chair, and the play continues with the third player making the second player an offer to get out of the chair. The first player goes to the back of the line.
- Play continues until all players have played at least twice.
- Avoid saying, "Gimme that chair!"

Examples

- "Your chair is on fire!"
- "I feel sick."
- "Your mother is calling you."
- "Look! Free food!"
- "Is that your dog?"

Focus Questions

- Were some offers more compelling than others?
- Were all of the exits motivated?
- Was it difficult to think of offers?
- Were there offers that just did not work? Why not?

This is one of the most effective games to play as it involves quick thinking, plot, and characterization. Kids *love* it. In improv, not accepting another player's offer is called blocking. For example, if a player says, "I feel sick," and the other player responds, "Go to the nurse," the other player is blocking the offer. A proper response would be, "You stay here and I'll get help."

Story, Story, Die

DEMO
0
MINUTES

PLAYER PREP
0
MINUTES

PERFORMANCE
20
MINUTES

Directions

- Director chooses five players to come to the front of the group.
- Each player is given a number (1-5).
- The entire group chooses a title for the story.
- Play starts with the director calling one of the players' numbers. That player starts telling the story.
- As soon as another number is called, the first player stops where he is in the story and the next player continues the story without a break.
- The next player cannot repeat, pause more than two seconds, or change the plot. If she does, then the group may call out "Die" and that player is out.
- The game continues with the director calling out numbers ever more rapidly until there is only one player left standing.
- Five more players and a new title are chosen, and the game begins again.

Focus Questions

- Was it difficult to pick up where the previous player left off?
- What techniques did you use to do this?
- Was it difficult to stay on the topic?
- Was it difficult to avoid using time fillers such as "and then," "and," and "uh"?
- Did the stories develop well?
- Were there titles that lent themselves more easily to development? Why?
- Was it difficult to develop a plot?

Type: Improv
Skill: Intermediate
Group Size: 5
Equipment: None

We play this game because:

By having to concentrate intensely on what is being said, we develop better concentration, observation, and creativity.

Emphasis:

Blocking and Conventions
Characterization
Concentration
Creativity
Ensemble Acting
Following Directions
Give and Take Focus
Group Dynamics
Listening and Silence
Memorization
Nonverbal Communication
Observation
Physical Control
Plot Structure
Spontaneity
Storytelling

Have ideas and/or titles on hand in case you get inappropriate suggestions. You can find a helpful list in *Improv Ideas*:
Film Titles — Page 61
Clichés — Pages 29-31
Fairy, Folk, and Children's Stories — Page 51
Generic Scenes — Page 71

Line at a Time

DEMO
0
MINUTES

PLAYER PREP
0
MINUTES

PERFORMANCE
10+
MINUTES

Type: Whole group
Skill: Beginning
Group Size: 10
Equipment: None

We play this game because:

It is a great warm-up and ice-breaker that encourages creativity and non-judgmental performance. (Just do it!)

Emphasis:

Blocking and Conventions

Characterization

Concentration

Creativity

Ensemble Acting

Following Directions

Give and Take Focus

Group Dynamics

Listening and Silence

Memorization

Nonverbal Communication

Observation

Physical Control

Plot Structure

Spontaneity

Storytelling

Directions

- Players form two equal lines facing each other.
- One at a time, a player from each side goes to the center and says a line for one of the topics called by the director.
- "Passing" is not an option. Players must say something, clever or not.
- Topics change whenever the director feels the energy ebbing.

Examples

Things that are Blue
- Blue (of *Blue's Clues*)
- Blue crayons
- The sky
- The ocean
- A sad mood

Excuses for being late
- I was attacked by a bear.
- Our house burned down.
- I broke my leg.
- I missed the bus.
- A plane crashed into my backyard.

Focus Questions

- Was it difficult to think of a response so quickly?
- Did you find yourself trying to think up a response in advance?
- Did you find yourself judging your own responses?
- Did it get easier to respond as the game went on?
- Were there creative responses?

Now is a good time to introduce the axiom that there are no wrong responses. When players blank, it's always fine for them to throw their hands up in the air and say "I feel stupid!" It breaks the tension.

Tell Me About the Time You ... (TMATTY)

DEMO **0** MINUTES   PLAYER PREP **0** MINUTES   PERFORMANCE **1** MINUTES

Type: Improv
Skill: Intermediate
Group Size: 1
Equipment: Chair or bench if desired

Directions

- One player faces the group.
- A one-minute time limit is given for the story.
- The director asks the player to "Tell me about the time you ..."
- Within the time limit, the player tells a personal (though fictional) story with a beginning, middle, and ending.
- The director or timekeeper signals thirty and fifteen seconds before the scene ends.

Hints for Success

- Try to catch our interest immediately. Perhaps ask a question to start. Perhaps make a provocative statement for starters.
- Develop the plot by describing a series of conflicts leading to a crisis.
- Make sure to start the conclusion by the time you have fifteen seconds left.

Focus Questions

- Was the player able to engage with the topic?
- Did the story have a beginning, middle, and end?
- Was there adequate development?
- Did the player convince you that this event really happened?

Challenges Players to Ramp It Up!

- Play this as an icebreaker.
- To pick up the pace, have the stories be thirty to forty-five seconds in length.
- Use a brief headline or magazine cover as a starter.

You can find a helpful list in *Improv Ideas*:
TMATTY Situations — Page 159

We play this game because:

This is a great warm-up and a speed game that encourages quick thinking under time constraints.

Emphasis:

Blocking and Conventions
Characterization
Concentration
Creativity
Ensemble Acting
Following Directions
Give and Take Focus
Group Dynamics
Listening and Silence
Memorization
Nonverbal Communication
Observation
Physical Control
Plot Structure
Spontaneity
Storytelling

Word Tennis

DEMO	PLAYER PREP	PERFORMANCE
3 MINUTES	**0** MINUTES	**10+** MINUTES

Type: Whole group/Improv
Skill: Beginning
Group Size: 2
Equipment: Ideas for categories

We play this game because:
Listening and thinking quickly on your feet are essential improvisation and acting skills.

Emphasis:

Blocking and Conventions

Characterization

Concentration

Creativity

Ensemble Acting

Following Directions

Give and Take Focus

Group Dynamics

Listening and Silence

Memorization

Nonverbal Communication

Observation

Physical Control

Plot Structure

Spontaneity

Storytelling

Directions

- Two players go to the front of the group. They take turns naming items in a given category quickly and accurately.
- They play until one hesitates, uses a stalling word, or repeats a formerly given item. It is up to the director how much hesitation is allowed. The director signals when there is a foul.
- The person who misses sits down and is replaced with a new player.
- A new category is given, and the game starts again.
- Play continues until all actors have had a turn or until time is up.
- Note categories for the next game.

Examples

Director: Languages
Actor 1: Spanish
Actor 2: English
Actor 1: Italian
Actor 2: French

Focus Questions

- Did the pace help or hurt your ability to respond?
- Were there specific techniques you used to respond quickly?

The director must be prepared with categories to use as categories change when each player is out. You can find a helpful list in
Improv Ideas:
Word Tennis Topics — Page 173

Beginning Improv

Lesson 25: Beginning Improv — Dialog

Emphasis: Working with lines of dialog as motivation for action.

Equipment: Index cards with dialog written on them.

Hint: *First Line, Last Line* encourages making quick plot and character decisions by incorporating the parameters of the two lines.

First Line, Last Line   **Minutes: 30**

Showing, not telling, is an essential part of learning to improvise and to act.

Whose Line   **Minutes: 20**

Having a conflict can really help relationships between characters.

Lesson 26: Beginning Improv — Accepting Offers

Emphasis: Continuing to accept offers and see how this can be the beginning of actual scene building.

Equipment: Benches

Hint: Go over types of relationships before playing *Park Bench*, as these may suggest scenes to the players.

Make Me Do It   **Minutes: 15**

Showing, not telling, is an essential part of learning to improvise and to act.

Park Bench   **Minutes: 15**

Having a conflict can really help create relationships between characters.

Twisted   **Minutes: 15**

A variation of *Park Bench*, *Twisted* emphasizes physical traits and conflict.

Beginning Improv (Continued)

Lesson 27: Beginning Improv — Ensemble

May take 2 class periods

Emphasis: Reacting and adapting quickly to new situations.

Equipment: Small objects

Hint: Allow for overflowing laughter and exaggeration! The humor keeps the flow going.

I've Got It, You Want It	**Minutes: 10**

Persuasion must involve convincing arguments as well as some honest emotional content.

Addition and Subtraction	**Minutes: 20**

Adapting quickly to new situations is the basis of all improvisational acting — accept all offers.

Happy Hands	**Minutes: 20-30**

We often express ourselves through particular parts of the body, which leads to our favoring of those parts (talking with hands, shuffling feet, tossing hair, etc.).

Lesson 28: Beginning Improv — Props

Emphasis: Working with props can mean with physical objects, or in this case, someone else's hands!

Equipment: Hats and headgear

Hint: *Gimme a Hand* is a great technique to break any ice still left and to really build confidence in working with a partner! *Hats* helps extend characterization.

Gimme a Hand	**Minutes: 20-30**

Voice and gestures need to work in harmony. (Plus this is just plain fun!)

Hats	**Minutes: 30**

Characters are often prompted or defined by what they wear.

First Line, Last Line

DEMO 5 MINUTES   **PLAYER PREP** 5 MINUTES   **PERFORMANCE** 1 MINUTES

Directions

- Divide into teams of two. Teams are divided into A's and B's.
- Player A is given a line to open with. Player B is given a line to close with.
- The audience supplies a location, title, or situation.
- Player A starts the scene with the opening line.
- The players develop the scene for about one minute.
- Player B ends the scene with the closing line.

Examples

Player A draws "You won't believe what happened today." The scene develops into a litany of woes that develop into real-time problems (sink plugging up, slipping on a banana peel, being bitten by a hamster, etc.) until Player B ends with his drawn last line, "Is it really over?"

Focus Questions

- Did the players establish a coherent scene that incorporated both lines?
- Were there clear characters?
- Did the scene have a beginning, middle, and ending?
- Were the lines motivated?

Challenge Players to Ramp It Up!

- The American Film Institute (www.afi.com) has four hundred film quotes — many of which would make wonderful first or last lines. (Look them over first!)

You can find a helpful list in *Improv Ideas*: First Line, Last Line — Pages 63-65

Type: Improv/Prepared
Skill: Beginning/Intermediate
Group Size: 2
Equipment: Index cards with opening and closing lines

We play this game because:
Learning to motivate actions and lines is a first step in becoming an actor.

Emphasis:

Blocking and Conventions
Characterization
Concentration
Creativity
Ensemble Acting
Following Directions
Give and Take Focus
Group Dynamics
Listening and Silence
Memorization
Nonverbal Communication
Observation
Physical Control
Plot Structure
Spontaneity
Storytelling

Whose Line

DEMO **5** MINUTES

PLAYER PREP **0** MINUTES

PERFORMANCE **10+** MINUTES

Type: Improv
Skill: Intermediate/Advanced
Group Size: 2
Equipment: Index cards
with dialog

We play this game because:
Learning to motivate even illogical/irrational lines into a scene expands the skills of the improviser.

Emphasis:

Blocking and Conventions

Characterization

Concentration

Creativity

Ensemble Acting

Following Directions

Give and Take Focus

Group Dynamics

Listening and Silence

Memorization

Nonverbal Communication

Observation

Physical Control

Plot Structure

Spontaneity

Storytelling

Directions

- Each player receives five to ten index cards of paper with lines of dialog on each. The players are not allowed to look at the lines in advance.
- The group suggests a title or generic scene.
- Players start the scene, establishing the who, where, and what.
- At random intervals each player turns over a card and incorporates the lines of dialog into the scene.

Focus Questions

- Were the players able to incorporate the lines into the scene so that the lines made sense and furthered the action?
- How did the actors motivate somewhat illogical lines into the action of the scene?

Discourage players from "setting up" the lines in advance. You can find a helpful list in
Improv Ideas:
Film Titles — Page 61
Generic Scenes — Page 71

Make Me Do It

DEMO	PLAYER PREP	PERFORMANCE
0 MINUTES	0 MINUTES	10+ MINUTES

Directions

- One player is chosen to be "It" and leaves the room.
- The class decides on an activity that another player will try to persuade It to do without directly stating what the activity is. (Show, don't tell!)
- It returns to the room and joins the persuader in front of the group.
- The persuader tries to get It to perform the activity without stating the activity or pantomiming it.
- When It thinks she knows what she is meant to do, she does it.

Examples

- Sing "I'm a Little Teapot."
- Say the Pledge of Allegiance.
- Sit on the stage.
- Scratch the persuader's back.
- Take off a shoe.

Focus Questions

- How did the persuader communicate what he wanted It to do?
- Were techniques of persuasion used?
- Was it difficult to avoid simply stating the request?
- How did It finally guess the activity?
- Did It cooperate or block?

Discuss how we manipulate others without them knowing it.

Type: Whole group
Skill: Beginning/Intermediate
Group Size: 2
Equipment: Furniture as needed

We play this game because:

Showing, not telling, is an essential part of learning to improvise and act.

Emphasis:

Blocking and Conventions
Characterization
Concentration
Creativity
Ensemble Acting
Following Directions
Give and Take Focus
Group Dynamics
Listening and Silence
Memorization
Nonverbal Communication
Observation
Physical Control
Plot Structure
Spontaneity
Storytelling

Park Bench

DEMO **0** MINUTES

PLAYER PREP **0** MINUTES

PERFORMANCE **10+** MINUTES

Type: Whole group/Improv
Skill: Intermediate
Group Size: 6
Equipment: A bench

We play this game because:

Having a conflict can really help create relationships between characters.

Emphasis:

Blocking and Conventions
Characterization
Concentration
Creativity
Ensemble Acting
Following Directions
Give and Take Focus
Group Dynamics
Listening and Silence
Memorization
Nonverbal Communication
Observation
Physical Control
Plot Structure
Spontaneity
Storytelling

Directions

- One player (Player A) sits at the far left corner of a bench.
- Five players line up at the right corner of the bench (Players B — F).
- Player A does not know who he is.
- Player B enters, sits next to Player A, and creates the identities of both of them.
- There should be no telling (show, don't tell). In other words, do not announce: "Hello, Principal Jones." Show by your interactions.
- As soon as Player A knows who he is, the players perform a ten-second scene. Player A finds a motivation for leaving, and Player B moves to the far left side of the bench.
- Player C now enters and creates identities as the play continues as above.
- The play continues with each player entering two or three times.

Examples

- Player B creates the scene in which A is the mother and B is a child late for dinner. A exits to get B's dinner.
- Player C creates a scene in which B is a famous movie star and C wants his autograph. B exits to get a pen.
- Player D creates a scene in which C is a victim and D is the robber. C exits, calling for help.

Focus Questions

- How difficult was it to generate ideas? How did you decide?
- How difficult was it to show, not tell?
- How did you let the first player know who he/she was?
- Was having a conflict important?
- How difficult was it to find a motivation to exit?
- Which relationships worked particularly well?
- Which relationships made it hard to create scenes?

You can find a helpful list in
Improv Ideas:
Status Relationships — Page 151

Twisted

DEMO
0
MINUTES

PLAYER PREP
0
MINUTES

PERFORMANCE
1/2
MINUTES

Type: Improv
Skill: Intermediate
Group Size: 3-7
Equipment: A bench

We play this game because:
This is a specifically physicalized variation of Park Bench.

Emphasis:

Blocking and Conventions
Characterization
Concentration
Creativity
Ensemble Acting
Following Directions
Give and Take Focus
Group Dynamics
Listening and Silence
Memorization
Nonverbal Communication
Observation
Physical Control
Plot Structure
Spontaneity
Storytelling

Directions

- One player sits in the playing area at the far end of a bench. Up to six players line up outside the playing area.
- One at a time, players from the group enter the scene and create an improbable physical trait for the seated player.
- The seated player (Player 1) accepts the newcomer's (Player 2) lead as to the where, when, why, and who of the scene, all the time trying to discover his unusual physical trait within the confines of the scene.
- When the seated player guesses what the trait is, he immediately assumes it and finds a motivation for exiting.
- Player 1 goes to the back of the line, and Player 2 sits on the bench.
- Play continues with the next player in line.

Examples

- Player 2 enters the scene as a robber planning a robbery with Player 1, who is endowed with being extremely short. By suggestion (show, don't tell), Player 2 explains how Player 1 will be useful as a decoy in the teller line at the bank. Player 1 leaves to get ready.
- Player 2 enters the scene as an aerobics instructor, endowing Player 1 with six double chins and admonishing him to do strenuous exercises. Player 1 chokes because his chins get in the way while doing push-ups. He stumbles out of the scene.

Focus Questions

- What kinds of interactions helped Player 1 guess his endowment?
- Did Player 2 show, not tell?
- When Player 1 guessed his endowment, did he physicalize it?
- Did the endowment motivate Player 1's exit?

Be careful not to make fun of physical disabilities — use fantasy ones.

I've Got It, You Want It

Type: Improv
Skill: Intermediate
Group Size: 2
Equipment: Small objects

We play this game because:

Persuasion must involve convincing arguments as well as some honest emotional content.

Emphasis:

Blocking and Conventions
Characterization
Concentration
Creativity
Ensemble Acting
Following Directions
Give and Take Focus
Group Dynamics
Listening and Silence
Memorization
Nonverbal Communication
Observation
Physical Control
Plot Structure
Spontaneity
Storytelling

Directions

- Two volunteers come to the front of the group.
- A is given an object (coin, pencil, stick, etc.), and B wants the object.
- The play begins immediately with A extolling the advantages of having the object and B trying to convince A to give the object to her.
- A should allow himself to be convinced only if the argument is really good.
- B cannot use force or trickery.
- Scenes usually last one minute.

Examples

A: I have this brand new Ticonderoga pencil. Isn't it a lovely yellow?
B: May I see it?
A: Why? Don't you have one?
B: No. On the way to school a car hit me and I lost all my school supplies.
A: Really? Are you hurt?
B: Yes. I just got back from the nurse's office and now I have to face Mr. Brown's test without my lucky pencil. Could I please borrow yours? Just for 5th period.
A: Well, (pause) OK.

Focus Questions

- What techniques of persuasion worked? Which ones didn't? Why?
- Was it easier to give in or hold on to the object?
- How did B sound sincere?

Discuss the use of persuasion in everyday life.

Addition and Subtraction

DEMO
5
MINUTES

PLAYER PREP
0
MINUTES

PERFORMANCE
15
MINUTES

Directions

- Five players are chosen to perform.
- The first player takes the stage and starts a simple scene.
- When the director calls "Freeze," another player enters and starts a completely new scene with the first player.
- When the director calls "Freeze" again, the third player enters and starts a new scene with players one and two.
- This continues until all five players have entered and started a scene.
- After the fifth player starts his new scene, he must find a motivation for leaving it.
- As soon as the fifth player leaves, the fourth player's scene resumes, and the fourth player leaves. This continues until the play ends back where it began.

Examples

- Scene one: A telephone conversation.
- Scene two: Two people baking a cake.
- Scene three: Three people in a classroom taking a test.
- Scene four: A game of tag.
- Scene five: A group of soldiers in the heat of battle.

Focus Questions

- Was it difficult to think of a new scene?
- Was it difficult to adapt to the new scene?
- Did all the players find a character to be in each scene?
- Did the exits seem motivated?
- Were the transitions from scene to scene smooth?

Type: Improv
Skill: Beginning/Intermediate
Group Size: 5
Equipment: None

We play this game because:

Adapting quickly to new situations is the basis of all improvisational acting — accept all offers!

Emphasis:

Blocking and Conventions

Characterization

Concentration

Creativity

Ensemble Acting

Following Directions

Give and Take Focus

Group Dynamics

Listening and Silence

Memorization

Nonverbal Communication

Observation

Physical Control

Plot Structure

Spontaneity

Storytelling

Happy Hands

DEMO
10
MINUTES

PLAYER PREP
0
MINUTES

PERFORMANCE
3
MINUTES

Type: Improv
Skill: Beginning
Group Size: 2
Equipment: None

We play this game because:

We express ourselves through particular parts of the body, often favoring certain parts (talking with hands, shuffling feet, tossing hair, etc.).

Emphasis:

Blocking and Conventions

Characterization

Concentration

Creativity

Ensemble Acting

Following Directions

Give and Take Focus

Group Dynamics

Listening and Silence

Memorization

Nonverbal Communication

Observation

Physical Control

Plot Structure

Spontaneity

Storytelling

Directions

- The group is to number off, one to four.
- The director tells the group that the ones are happy, twos are sad, threes are angry, and fours are confused. They are to keep these emotions to themselves.
- The director then asks them to scramble and number off again, one to four.
- Now the director informs the group that the ones are hands, the twos are feet, the threes are heads, and the fours are bottoms. They are to keep these body parts to themselves.
- Each player now has an emotion and a body part (sad head, happy hands, angry feet, etc.).
- Two volunteers come to the front of the group. The situation is a job interview. One player is chosen to be the interviewer; the other is the interviewee.
- The scene begins with each player exaggerating his/her emotion and body part — but not to the extent that it does not seem natural.
- After about a minute, the scene is frozen and the group is asked to guess each player's emotion and body part.
- New players are chosen and another scene begins.

Focus Questions

- What parts of the body were easiest to use?
- What parts of the body were more awkward?
- What emotions were easiest? Hardest?
- What were some of the creative but realistic ways these were improvised?
- How did the emotions determine the plot?

This is one of the most effective games to play, as it involves quick thinking, plot, and characterization. Kids *love* it!

Gimme a Hand

DEMO
0
MINUTES

PLAYER PREP
0
MINUTES

PERFORMANCE
5
MINUTES

Directions

- Two players volunteer to play a generic scene.
- Two other players volunteer to be the first two players' hands. (Try to match players by gender and size, as the smaller player will stand behind the taller player. The taller player's hands will be behind her back.)
- The players who are the hands will gesture for the speaking players, following the words and actions of the speaking players.
- *Or,* one player speaks to the group with another standing behind as the hands.

Focus Questions

- Did the hands match the words?
- Did the hands upstage the voice, or did they work together?
- Did the hands create comedy? If so, why?
- Did this work, or was it distracting?

Type: Improv
Skill: Beginning
Group Size: 4
Equipment: None

We play this game because:
*Voice and gestures need
to work in harmony.
(Plus this is just plain fun!)*

Emphasis:

Blocking and Conventions

Characterization

Concentration

Creativity

Ensemble Acting

Following Directions

Give and Take Focus

Group Dynamics

Listening and Silence

Memorization

Nonverbal Communication

Observation

Physical Control

Plot Structure

Spontaneity

Storytelling

Avoid letting the players just be silly unless you only need a time filler. You can find a helpful list in *Improv Ideas*: Generic Scenes — Page 71

Hats

DEMO
5
MINUTES

PLAYER PREP
10+
MINUTES

PERFORMANCE
1-3
MINUTES

Type: Prepared
Skill: Beginning
Group Size: 3-5
Equipment: A variety of hats and headgear

We play this game because:

Characters are often prompted or defined by what they wear.

Emphasis:

Blocking and Conventions

Characterization

Concentration

Creativity

Ensemble Acting

Following Directions

Give and Take Focus

Group Dynamics

Listening and Silence

Memorization

Nonverbal Communication

Observation

Physical Control

Plot Structure

Spontaneity

Storytelling

Display

An assortment of hats and headgear as players enter.

Discuss

How one can observe/assume many things about people by what they wear.

Directions

- Each player chooses a hat.
- Divide the players into groups of three to five.
- Players have ten to fifteen minutes to create a one- to three-minute scene based on characters suggested by the hats.

Focus Questions

- Were the characters prompted by the hats?
- Was conflict prompted by the characters?
- Did the scene have a beginning, a middle, and an ending?

Players may take possession of the hat and wear it during planning and performance; plan without the hat and wear it during the performance; or plan and perform without wearing the hat at all. The last option is excellent if there is a concern about sanitation or head lice.

Vocal Improv

Lesson 29: Vocal Improvisation I

Emphasis: Limiting the use of language to see how vocal tone alone can carry meaning.

Equipment: None

Hint: Be sure to brainstorm the latest slang for the players to use, as it seems to change daily! Also note regional/ethnic slang.

Yes/No — One Word Scenes   Minutes: 15
Even though dialog is restricted to one word, that one word can carry an enormous variety of meanings.

In a Manner of Speaking   Minutes: 30-40
Using known clichés as prompts stretches the imagination and encourages us to look at our own communication.

Lesson 30: Vocal Improvisation II

Emphasis: Continuing to stretch our vocal capabilities by playing more word-limiting games.

Equipment: None

Hint: Players who know another language always want to use it in these games. Make them invent something new and different. Often, limiting options can open up new avenues to creativity!

Exchange Student/Translators   Minutes: 15
Reacting to sound and movement requires a great deal of concentration, not just cleverness.

Gibberish   Minutes: 15
Without the use of words, vocal variety becomes essential to carry meaning.

Alphabet Game   Minutes: 20
Being restricted to starting each sentence with a different letter of the alphabet stretches the creative imagination.

Yes/No — One-Word Scenes

DEMO
0
MINUTES

PLAYER PREP
0
MINUTES

PERFORMANCE
10+
MINUTES

Type: Improv
Skill: Beginning/Intermediate
Group Size: 2
Equipment: None

We play this game because:

Even though dialog is restricted to one word, that one word can carry an enormous variety of meanings.

Emphasis:

Blocking and Conventions

Characterization

Concentration

Creativity

Ensemble Acting

Following Directions

Give and Take Focus

Group Dynamics

Listening and Silence

Memorization

Nonverbal Communication

Observation

Physical Control

Plot Structure

Spontaneity

Storytelling

Directions

- Two players volunteer and come to the front of the group.
- Player A can only say "Yes."
- Player B can only say "No."
- The group may give a plot or title, but in a more experienced group we recommend that the scene start immediately with player A's "yes."
- The play continues until the scene is finished, about one minute.
- Note that players should use only "yes" and "no," but they may use variants such as "yeah" and "nah."
- Note also that the players are not limited to using the words once. See example.

Examples

- Player A says "Yes?" Indicating some object in front of her.
- Player B looks at it quizzically and finally says, "No."
- Player A proceeds to another object, examines it, hands it to B and pronounces: "Yes!"
- B immediately throws it down, saying "No!" in disgust.

Focus Questions

- Did the words "yes" and "no" limit you?
- How did you avoid a ping-pong type argument/fight/debate?
- How did you use the same word in different ways?
- Was the group clear on the who, where, and what of the scene?
- How did the players decide on an ending?
- Did it end on a yes or a no?
- Was the scene effective?

In a Manner of Speaking

DEMO 0 MINUTES

PLAYER PREP 0 MINUTES

PERFORMANCE 3 MINUTES

Directions

- Divide into teams of two.
- Each player thinks of, draws, or is assigned at least five clichés.
- The audience suggests a who and where.
- The improv starts immediately. Players improvise a two-minute scene with a beginning, middle, and ending in which they incorporate the clichés into the dialog.

Examples

- Shoppers at a once-a-year sale.
- Students taking the ACT or SAT.
- Guests at a wedding.
- Mourners at a funeral.

Focus Questions

- Were the clichés able to be incorporated into the plot in a logical manner?
- Was the plot coherent?
- Was there a beginning, a middle, and an ending?

Type: Improv
Skill: Intermediate/Advanced
Group Size: 2
Equipment: None

We play this game because:

Using known clichés as prompts stretches the imagination and encourages us to look at our own communication.

Emphasis:

Blocking and Conventions
Characterization
Concentration
Creativity
Ensemble Acting
Following Directions
Give and Take Focus
Group Dynamics
Listening and Silence
Memorization
Nonverbal Communication
Observation
Physical Control
Plot Structure
Spontaneity
Storytelling

Discuss well-known clichés before you play the game. You can find a helpful list in *Improv Ideas*:
Clichés (and Tired Phrases) — Pages 29-31

Exchange Student/Translators

Type: Whole group
Skill: Beginning
Group Size: 2
Equipment: None

We play this game because:

The use of gibberish can free the players vocally! Also, listening emotionally and intuitively is an important skill.

Emphasis:

Blocking and Conventions

Characterization

Concentration

Creativity

Ensemble Acting

Following Directions

Give and Take Focus

Group Dynamics

Listening and Silence

Memorization

Nonverbal Communication

Observation

Physical Control

Plot Structure

Spontaneity

Storytelling

Directions

- Two volunteers are chosen. One is the exchange student; one is the translator.
- The exchange student addresses the group in gibberish, her "native language."
- After each pause, the translator tells the group what has just been said.
- The exchange student must go with what the translator interprets as the address continues.

Focus Questions

- What did the gibberish sound like to you? Did it develop the character?
- Did the gibberish maintain a variety of emotional content?
- Could you tell what the exchange student was trying to communicate?
- Did the translator seem to truly understand what was being said?
- Did the translator and the exchange student work in harmony?

Be sure to let the exchange student speak more than one sentence before each translation; otherwise the game will be too slow.

Gibberish

DEMO
0
MINUTES

PLAYER PREP
0
MINUTES

PERFORMANCE
10+
MINUTES

Directions

- Two players volunteer and come to the front of the group.
- The group gives the players a situation.
- Player A starts the scene, but speaks only in gibberish.
- Player B responds, also in gibberish.
- The scene progresses until finished, and should last at least thirty seconds.

Focus Questions

- When given a plot or title, how did you decide on your character?
- How did this character determine who the other character would be?
- Was it difficult for Player B to discover or create who he should be in the scene?
- How did A feel if B created a character or situation that was not what A expected?
- Could the players understand what was going on? Could the group?
- Was there a conflict?
- How did the conflict help the plot?
- Did the use of gibberish help or hinder the scene?
- What compensations were made for lack of words?

Type: Improv
Skill: Intermediate
Group Size: 2
Equipment: None

We play this game because:
Without the use of words, vocal variety becomes essential to carry meaning.

Emphasis:

Blocking and Conventions
Characterization
Concentration
Creativity
Ensemble Acting
Following Directions
Give and Take Focus
Group Dynamics
Listening and Silence
Memorization
Nonverbal Communication
Observation
Physical Control
Plot Structure
Spontaneity
Storytelling

Some players are tempted to use a second language. Make sure they actually make up gibberish on the spot. You can find a helpful list in *Improv Ideas*: Generic Scenes — Page 71

Alphabet Game

DEMO 0 MINUTES **PLAYER PREP** 0 MINUTES **PERFORMANCE** 15+ MINUTES

Type: Improv
Skill: Intermediate
Group Size: 2
Equipment: None

We play this game because:

Being restricted to starting each sentence with a different letter of the alphabet stretches the creative imagination.

Emphasis:

Blocking and Conventions
Characterization
Concentration
Creativity
Ensemble Acting
Following Directions
Give and Take Focus
Group Dynamics
Listening and Silence
Memorization
Nonverbal Communication
Observation
Physical Control
Plot Structure
Spontaneity
Storytelling

Directions

- Two volunteers come to the front of the group.
- A random person calls out a letter of the alphabet.
- Player A must start a scene or a story with the letter provided. (Example: R. "Right! I think we go left at the next corner.")
- Player B continues the scene with the next letter of the alphabet. ("Susan said it was right, not left!")
- The play continues until one of the players is stumped or the scene or story comes back to the initial letter.

Examples

(Starting with A)
- "As you can see, this is a very difficult problem."
- "But I think we can solve it."
- "Can we?"
- "Don't be discouraged."
- "Everyone says it's impossible."
- "Fine! Quit if you want."
- "Great! Throw a hissy fit!"
- "How can you say that?"
- "It's obvious."
- "Just a minute." (By this time they need to establish what the problem is.)
- "Keeping rattlesnakes as pets is just too dangerous — even for our science project."

Focus Questions

- Did the players stay on topic?
- Did the players keep up the pace?
- Was the scene motivated?
- Did the letters of the alphabet restrict the play?
- How did players deal with difficult letters?
- What stumped them?

It is often difficult to get on topic. Try not to spend too much time generalizing, avoiding, or building up to the topic.

Unit 14:
Where Are We?

Lesson 31: Where Improvs I

Emphasis: Focusing on using the "where" to create improv scenes.

Equipment: Levels, benches, chairs

Hint: These games can seem to require a great deal of pantomime skill. To alleviate concerns in this area, stress that players need only suggest the scene "roughly."

The Where Game   Minutes: 15-20
A "where" is made up of many subtle parameters such as entrances and exits, furniture, objects, etc. Defining these parameters gives performers much more with which to work.

Add a Where   Minutes: 15-20
Situations often have to adapt to the locale.

Lesson 32: Where Improvs II

Emphasis: Using the basic "where" concept and adding other factors to make the improv even more specific.

Equipment: None

Hint: Make sure players clearly establish the "where" before adding the other elements.

In a ... With A ...   Minutes: 15-20
Using a where and an object can help performers design an improv.

In a ... With A ... While A ...   Minutes: 15-20
Adding a weather condition gives performers even more material with which to work.

The Where Game

DEMO
5
MINUTES

PLAYER PREP
0
MINUTES

PERFORMANCE
10+
MINUTES

Type: Whole group
Skill: Beginning
Group Size: Whole group
Equipment: None

We play this game because:

A "where" is made up of many subtle parameters such as entrances and exits, furniture, objects, etc. Defining these gives performers much more to work with.

Emphasis:

Blocking and Conventions

Characterization

Concentration

Creativity

Ensemble Acting

Following Directions

Give and Take Focus

Group Dynamics

Listening and Silence

Memorization

Nonverbal Communication

Observation

Physical Control

Plot Structure

Spontaneity

Storytelling

Directions

- The group stands in a large circle.
- One player thinks or, draws, or is assigned the name of a fantasy or real location.
- The player goes to the center of the circle and starts an activity associated with that location.
- One at a time, other players come in and add to the scene by establishing other landmarks in the location. Each player furthers the plot.

Examples

- The location is a cemetery. The first player enters and begins digging a grave. Other players come in putting flowers near headstones and mowing around the graves.
- The location is a playground. The first player enters and begins playing in a sandbox. Other players join in by swinging on the swings or playing on a teeter-totter.

Focus Questions

- How many players did it take to establish the location?
- Once established, how did the location contribute to the plot?
- Was there a beginning, middle, and ending, or did the scene just keeping adding items to the location?
- Were any pantomimed physical items used after their creation?
- Were the items used imaginatively to further the plot?

This basic game which emphasizes essential skills may be repeated throughout the course. You can find a helpful list in *Improv Ideas*:
Places — Pages 119-121
Rooms in a House — Page 135
Enclosed Spaces — Page 39
Character Traits — Pages 24-27

Add a Where

DEMO
0
MINUTES

PLAYER PREP
0
MINUTES

PERFORMANCE
15+
MINUTES

Directions

- Two volunteers come to the front.
- A generic scene is drawn or suggested.
- Players start the scene. After approximately thirty seconds, the director calls out a where.
- The players adapt the scene to fit the location.
- After another thirty seconds the director calls out a new where, and the players logically adapt the scene to fit the new where.
- The director goes through three or four wheres, switching every thirty to sixty seconds depending on the experience of the players.

Focus Questions

- Were the wheres physicalized?
- Were the wheres used to add more interest to the scene?
- Did the wheres make the situations clearer? If so, how?
- Were the switches in where clear?

This game can be played by the whole class divided into pairs — having one generic scene for all pairs and having each pair draw a different "where." You can find a helpful list in *Improv Ideas*: Generic Scenes — Page 71

Type: Improv
Skill: Intermediate/Advanced
Group Size: 2
Equipment: Chairs, benches, levels

We play this game because:
Situations often have to adapt to the locale.

Emphasis:

Blocking and Conventions
Characterization
Concentration
Creativity
Ensemble Acting
Following Directions
Give and Take Focus
Group Dynamics
Listening and Silence
Memorization
Nonverbal Communication
Observation
Physical Control
Plot Structure
Spontaneity
Storytelling

In A ... With A ...

Type: Improv
Skill: Intermediate
Group Size: 2
Equipment: None

We play this game because:

This game incorporates both a where and a what into one improvisation.

Emphasis:

Blocking and Conventions
Characterization
Concentration
Creativity
Ensemble Acting
Following Directions
Give and Take Focus
Group Dynamics
Listening and Silence
Memorization
Nonverbal Communication
Observation
Physical Control
Plot Structure
Spontaneity
Storytelling

Directions

- Divide into teams of two.
- The teams are assigned or draw the name of a place and an object.
- The players have a set amount of time (one to three minutes is usually sufficient) to act out a scene that uses the object and place. The scene must have a coherent plot that contains a beginning, a middle, and an ending.
- The director or a timer alerts the players when there are ten seconds remaining in the allotted improv time.

Examples

- In a Tibetan monastery with a marble.
- In a pirate ship with a feather.

Focus Questions

- How was the where established?
- Were details of the location used?
- Was the where clear?
- Did the location further the plot?
- Did the object further the plot? Add a conflict? Provide a solution?
- Were there clearly defined characters?
- Was there a clear beginning, middle, and ending?

It is sometimes necessary to "model" these games to show how it is possible to establish location immediately.
You can find a helpful list in *Improv Ideas*:
Objects — Page 101
Places — Pages 119-121

In A ... With A ... While A ...

Type: Improv
Skill: Intermediate/Advanced
Group Size: 2
Equipment: None

Directions

- Divide into teams of two.
- The teams are assigned or draw the name of a place, an object, and an event or weather condition.
- The players have a set amount of time (one to three minutes is usually sufficient) to act out a scene that uses the object, the place, and the event or weather condition. The scene must have a coherent plot that contains a beginning, a middle, and an ending.
- The director or a timer alerts the players when there are ten seconds remaining in the allotted improv time.

Examples

- In a rowboat, with an eraser, while a total eclipse of the sun takes place.
- In a prison, with a jump rope, during the Russian revolution.
- In a spaceship, with a lava lamp, while a garbage strike is underway.

Focus Questions

- Were the where, what, and while established quickly and completely?
- Did the where, what, and while significantly impact the ending?
- Was there a beginning, middle, and ending?
- Were characters well developed?
- Was the conflict well developed?

We play this game because:

Adding a third conflicting situation to the scene really stretches the improvisers' creativity.

Emphasis:

Blocking and Conventions
Characterization
Concentration
Creativity
Ensemble Acting
Following Directions
Give and Take Focus
Group Dynamics
Listening and Silence
Memorization
Nonverbal Communication
Observation
Physical Control
Plot Structure
Spontaneity
Storytelling

Students always enjoy exaggerating the weather conditions. Try not to let this get out of hand. You can find a helpful list in *Improv Ideas*:

Objects — Page 101

Places — Pages 119-121

Weather — Page 169

Unit 15:
Sound Off

Lesson 33: Speech Exercises I

May take 2 class periods.

Emphasis: Playing basic speech games to stretch the intellect and encourage spontaneity.

Equipment: Paper and pencils

Hint: These particular speech games are often competitive events, but in this context they are fun activities for quick thinking "outside the box."

Impromptu   **Minutes: 20**

Learning to organize thoughts into a coherent whole is a critical impromptu skill.

SPAR (Spontaneous Argumentation)   **Minutes: 40**

Debating a "light" subject can help players learn to effectively plan convincing and objective arguments.

Lesson: 34: Speech Exercises II

Emphasis: Performing personification monologs.

Equipment: Paper and pencils

Hint: Take a look around the playing space and list some of the objects in the room. These can include walls, floors, and ceilings! Then "model" attitudes for each before giving the assignment.

I'm a Little Teapot   **Minutes: 50-60**

Giving voice to inanimate objects can greatly enhance the understanding of emotional qualities in humans.

Impromptu

DEMO
3-5
MINUTES

PLAYER PREP
1/2
MINUTES

PERFORMANCE
1-2
MINUTES

Directions

- A volunteer comes to the front of the group.
- The director gives the player the name of an object or a concept (see examples).
- The player has thirty seconds to think of and organize a one- to two-minute talk on the given subject.

Examples

- Time
- Discipline
- Rap music
- Dogs
- Spiders

Focus Questions

- Was there an engaging introduction that immediately got our attention?
- Were there at least two points developed?
- Was there a conclusion that wrapped up the talk?
- Did the player seem energetic?
- Did the player seem involved with the subject?
- Was the talk well organized?

Type: Improv
Skill: Intermediate
Group Size: 1
Equipment: None

We play this game because:

Learning to organize thoughts into a coherent whole is a critical impromptu and life skill.

Emphasis:

Blocking and Conventions

Characterization

Concentration

Creativity

Ensemble Acting

Following Directions

Give and Take Focus

Group Dynamics

Listening and Silence

Memorization

Nonverbal Communication

Observation

Physical Control

Plot Structure

Spontaneity

Storytelling

The director must be prepared to demonstrate from group suggestions.

SPAR (Spontaneous Argumentation)

DEMO
10
MINUTES

PLAYER PREP
15
MINUTES

PERFORMANCE
6
MINUTES

Type: Improv
Skill: Intermediate/Advanced
Group Size: 2
Equipment: Paper and pencils

We play this game because:

Debating a "light" subject can help players learn to effectively plan convincing and objective arguments.

Emphasis:

Blocking and Conventions

Characterization

Concentration

Creativity

Ensemble Acting

Following Directions

Give and Take Focus

Group Dynamics

Listening and Silence

Memorization

Nonverbal Communication

Observation

Physical Control

Plot Structure

Spontaneity

Storytelling

Directions

- Choose two players to SPAR. Players come to the front of the group and are assigned affirmative (pro) or negative (con) sides.
- Players are given a resolution (topic).
- The pro player gets one minute to state her opening arguments.
- The con player gets one minute to state his opening arguments.
- The pro player gets one minute to rebut the con player's opening arguments.
- The con player gets one minute to rebut the pro player's opening arguments.
- The pro player gets one minute to make a closing statement.
- The con player gets one minute to make a closing statement.
- The rest of the group critiques.

Examples

Girls are superior to boys.
- Pro ideas: Girls get higher SAT scores. Girls get better grades. Girls are less violent.
- Con ideas: Boys are stronger. Historically boys have almost always been the movers and shakers in the world. Many religions recognize males as the power centers.

Focus Questions

- What persuasive techniques were used?
- Which were effective?
- Which didn't work?

Be very clear about the difference between *argumentation* and *argument*. See Persuasion and Propaganda Techniques in the Appendix (page 212). You can find a helpful list in *Improv Ideas*:
SPAR Topics — Page 149

I'm a Little Teapot

DEMO
5
MINUTES

PLAYER PREP
10
MINUTES

PERFORMANCE
1
MINUTES

Directions

- Each player gets the name of an object on a slip of paper, a blank piece paper, and a pencil.
- Players are given ten minutes to prepare an interior monolog as if they were the objects. Monologs should have a specific attitude and plot.
- Players then perform their one-minute monologs for the group.

Examples

- A clock complains that it is always stared at by people and that no one ever really sees him for who he is.
- A chair feels abused because students in the classroom plop down on it and lean back so far that it almost breaks every day.

Focus Questions

- Did the object have a personality?
- Did the object tell its story with emotion or attitude?
- Was there a story to tell?
- Did the story have a beginning, a middle, and an ending?
- Did the vocal quality and gestures fit the characterization?

Challenge players to Ramp It Up!

Play *I'm a Little Teapot* as an improv — no prep time!

You can find a helpful list in *Improv Ideas*: Objects — Page 101

Type: Prepared
Skill: Intermediate
Group Size: 1
Equipment: Paper and pencil for each player

We play this game because:

Giving voice to inanimate objects can greatly enhance understanding of emotional qualities in humans.

Emphasis:

Blocking and Conventions
Characterization
Concentration
Creativity
Ensemble Acting
Following Directions
Give and Take Focus
Group Dynamics
Listening and Silence
Memorization
Nonverbal Communication
Observation
Physical Control
Plot Structure
Spontaneity
Storytelling

This Is Rank

Lesson 35: Status

Emphasis: Introducing the concept of status and how all relationships contain some form of status.

Equipment: Benches, cards numbered 1-10

Hint: Before starting the class, have all students freeze and observe each other's postures. Make a connection between postures and status.

Status Bench   **Minutes: 60**

Status is determined by societal roles, body position, and self-esteem.

Lesson 36: Changing Status

Emphasis: Continuing an understanding of status.

Equipment: Chairs

Hint: Have students observe their own and others' postures and relate those ideas to the concept of status.

Master Servant   **Minutes: 30**

Exaggerating aspects of high and low status in a comic scene.

Status Slide   **Minutes: 30**

Starting at one end of a spectrum and then gradually shifting to the other end gives insight into both the obvious and the more subtle differences in status.

Status Bench

DEMO
0
MINUTES

PLAYER PREP
0
MINUTES

PERFORMANCE
5+
MINUTES

Type: Improv
Skill: Intermediate/Advanced
Group Size: 10
Equipment: Benches, cards numbered 1-10

Directions

- Ten players sit on benches in front of the group.
- Each player is given a number from one to ten on a card. One is the lowest status and ten the highest.
- Players assume body language that they associate with their given status levels.
- The group asks the players questions to try to guess their status levels.
- After all players have been interviewed at least twice, a volunteer tries to re-group the bench players from lowest to highest status.
- Players then reveal their numbers.

Examples

- What is your occupation?
- How many years did you go to school?
- What are your hobbies?
- What is your yearly income?

Focus Questions

- Did the body language help determine status?
- What questions were the most effective in determining status levels?
- How were slight changes in status shown?

We play this game because:
Status is determined by societal roles, body position, and self-esteem.

Emphasis:

Blocking and Conventions
Characterization
Concentration
Creativity
Ensemble Acting
Following Directions
Give and Take Focus
Group Dynamics
Listening and Silence
Memorization
Nonverbal Communication
Observation
Physical Control
Plot Structure
Spontaneity
Storytelling

Laminate large cards numbered from 1 to 10 to use with this and other exercises.

Master Servant

DEMO
2
MINUTES

PLAYER PREP
0
MINUTES

PERFORMANCE
2-3
MINUTES

Type: Improv
Skill: Intermediate
Group Size: 2
Equipment: None

We play this game because:

Exaggeration in the extreme is an easy way to break the ice and explore characterization.

Emphasis:

Blocking and Conventions

Characterization

Concentration

Creativity

Ensemble Acting

Following Directions

Give and Take Focus

Group Dynamics

Listening and Silence

Memorization

Nonverbal Communication

Observation

Physical Control

Plot Structure

Spontaneity

Storytelling

Directions

- Two volunteers come to the front of the group. One is the master and the other is the servant.
- Decide on a where for the scene (castle, drawing room in Britain, kitchen, galley of a ship, etc.).
- The scene starts with the master instructing the servant in some task.
- As the scene progresses the master becomes more and more high status as the servant's status sinks lower and lower.
- The director calls "Cut" when the scene has reached a logical climax or conclusion.

Focus Questions

- How did the master show her high status?
- How did the servant show his low status?
- Were the statuses progressively exaggerated?
- Did the players react appropriately in their respective statuses?
- How did the players' statuses contribute to the plot?
- How did the status of the players contribute to the conclusion (if there was one)?

Play with the physicalization of the characters (the high status can be regal, the low bumbling, etc.)

Status Slide

DEMO	PLAYER PREP	PERFORMANCE
5 MINUTES	**0** MINUTES	**5** MINUTES

Directions

- Divide into teams of two.
- Each pair draws or is assigned a relationship. Each relationship has a traditionally higher-status person and a traditionally lower-status person (master/servant).
- Each pair plans a scene in which the players emphasize their expected relationships. The higher-status player always puts the lower-status player down and raises himself. The lower-status player should lower himself while raising the higher-status player.
- Each pair performs for the group.
- At some time during the action, the director calls out, "Switch!"
- Although the players keep their same characters, they must slowly switch status until both are completely opposite from the way they started.

Focus Questions

- How did the players physicalize the characters' status?
- Did physical/vocal traits change as the status changed?
- Could you make some general statements about the physical differences between high- and low-status characters?

This game can get really wild. Make sure no one is allowed to make physical contact. Also be certain that your players understand this is "just for fun."

Type: Improv
Skill: Intermediate/Advanced
Group Size: 2
Equipment: Chairs

We play this game because:

Starting at one end of a spectrum and then gradually shifting to the other end gives insight into both the obvious and the more subtle differences in status.

Emphasis:

Blocking and Conventions
Characterization
Concentration
Creativity
Ensemble Acting
Following Directions
Give and Take Focus
Group Dynamics
Listening and Silence
Memorization
Nonverbal Communication
Observation
Physical Control
Plot Structure
Spontaneity
Storytelling

I Give You This — Endowments

Lesson 37: Endowments I

Emphasis: Exaggerating characterizations through improv games.

Equipment: Chairs, tables, stools

Hint: These games are among the most popular ever! They are usually played for broad laughs. Later you may want to go for more subtle characterization.

Party Quirk Endowments	**Minutes: 30**

This reinforces endowment and characterization skills in a fun and inclusive way.

Obsessed With	**Minutes: 30**

Obsessions can be a form or motivation carrying forward the plot and aspects of a character's personality.

Lesson 38: Endowments II

Emphasis: Using occupations and illnesses to define characters.

Equipment: Stools, benches

Hint: Be sure to discuss how an occupation and a physical condition can physicalize a character.

What's My Line?	**Minutes: 20**

Occupations often help define characters' personalities.

Sick	**Minutes: 30-40**

We want to see how illnesses affect a character's physical and emotional state.

I Give You This — Endowments (Continued)

Lesson 39: Endowments III

Emphasis: Making values explicit adds depth to characters.

Equipment: Chairs, tables, stools

Hint: Let players discuss the differences between primary/secondary and implicit/explicit values. (See Appendix, page 213.)

Values   Minutes: 50-60

Values help determine who we are as human beings.

Lesson 40: Endowments IV

Emphasis: Playing these games as more extensions on the use of endowments in improvisation.

Equipment: Chairs, benches, stools

Hint: The game show format is a lot of fun and a non-threatening way to play with endowments.

You've Got a Secret   Minutes: 20-30

Endowing players with personality traits and having them guess helps improvisers respond quickly and appropriately.

Roommate   Minutes: 20-30

Having roommates (or siblings) is a familiar situation for most.

Party Quirk Endowments

DEMO
0
MINUTES

PLAYER PREP
0
MINUTES

PERFORMANCE
5
MINUTES

Type: Improv
Skill: Intermediate
Group Size: 5
Equipment: Chairs,
tables, stools

We play this game because:

This is a fun and inclusive way to reinforce endowment and characterization skills.

Emphasis:

Blocking and Conventions

Characterization

Concentration

Creativity

Ensemble Acting

Following Directions

Give and Take Focus

Group Dynamics

Listening and Silence

Memorization

Nonverbal Communication

Observation

Physical Control

Plot Structure

Spontaneity

Storytelling

Directions

- Divide into teams of five. One player is chosen to be the host of a party. The four other players are guests.
- The host leaves the room.
- Each one of the guests is endowed with a quirk. This may be drawn from a box or assigned by the group or director while the host is out of earshot. (Note: Usually the rest of the group is aware of the endowments.)
- The host starts the party. As each guest arrives, he plays his quirk as a natural part of his personality.
- The host gradually amasses enough information during the course of the party to guess each guest's quirk.
- When the host guesses, she acknowledges the quirk as part of the scene and continues to guess the rest.

Focus Questions

- Were the guests able to play the quirks without giving them away too easily? (Show, don't tell.)
- Did the quirks direct the guests' personalities?
- How did the quirks add to the life of the party?
- Were the quirks compatible or did they cause conflicts?

Challenge Players to Ramp It Up!

Have the host secretly endow the guests with quirks that they must guess.

Watch *Whose Line Is It, Anyway?* to see how the pros do it. You can find a helpful list in *Improv Ideas*: Quirks — Page 129

Obsessed With

DEMO
0
MINUTES

PLAYER PREP
3
MINUTES

PERFORMANCE
5
MINUTES

Directions

- Divide into teams of two.
- The players think of, draw, or are assigned an obsession.
- The group gives the players a place, a cliché, or a title for the scene.
- Players have three minutes to plan and set up for the scene.
- As the scene progresses the players gradually become more and more obsessed.

Examples

- The players met in a hospital ER. A, the doctor, is obsessed with the news on TV. B, a nurse, is obsessed with nitpicking. While on an unauthorized break, A is glued to the TV while B tries to interest him in her constant complaints about the other doctors, nurses, and patients.
- The players act out a title, "The Phone Call." A and B are sisters. A is obsessed with having secrets, so she is trying not to let B, obsessed with gossip, listen to her call to her boyfriend.

Focus Questions

- How were the obsessions incorporated into the characters' personalities?
- Did the obsessions determine or contribute to the plot?

Discuss the obsessions of characters in well-known TV shows. You can find a helpful list in *Improv Ideas*:
Places — Pages 119-121
Film Titles — Page 61
Clichés (and Tired Phrases) — Page 29
Obsessions — Page 103

Type: Prepared
Skill: Intermediate/Advanced
Group Size: 2
Equipment: Furniture

We play this game because:

Obsessions can be a form or motivation in carrying forward the plot and aspects of a character's personality.

Emphasis:

Blocking and Conventions
Characterization
Concentration
Creativity
Ensemble Acting
Following Directions
Give and Take Focus
Group Dynamics
Listening and Silence
Memorization
Nonverbal Communication
Observation
Physical Control
Plot Structure
Spontaneity
Storytelling

DEMO
2 MINUTES

PLAYER PREP
0 MINUTES

PERFORMANCE
5 MINUTES

Type: Improv
Skill: Intermediate/Advanced
Group Size: 4
Equipment: Stools, benches

We play this game because:
Occupations often help define characters' personalities.

Emphasis:

Blocking and Conventions
Characterization
Concentration
Creativity
Ensemble Acting
Following Directions
Give and Take Focus
Group Dynamics
Listening and Silence
Memorization
Nonverbal Communication
Observation
Physical Control
Plot Structure
Spontaneity
Storytelling

Directions

- Divide into teams of four. The director chooses one player from the team to be the host.
- Each of the remaining three players is endowed with an occupation that only the group and the host know.
- One at a time the players enter the talk show scene and are interviewed about their jobs. Since the players do not know what their jobs are, the answers can be quite humorous.
- Players must try to adapt to reactions to their answers, eventually discovering their endowed occupations.

Focus Questions

- What kinds of questions were the most useful to the players?
- What kinds of questions were superfluous?
- When the players guessed their occupations, how did they physicalize them, if at all?

You can find a helpful list in *Improv Ideas*:
Occupations — Pages 105-107

Sick

DEMO
2
MINUTES

PLAYER PREP
1-2
MINUTES

PERFORMANCE
1-2
MINUTES

Directions

- Divide into teams of two.
- Each player draws an illness.
- Without knowing the illnesses, the audience chooses a situation, relationship, generic scene, or title for the scene.
- Players improvise a scene in which each character has an illness. The type of illness determines the plot.

Examples

Blind Date: The male has acne and the female has a hearing loss. At first they are mutually disappointed with the date, but as they learn more about each other, they learn to appreciate each other in spite of "imperfections."

Focus Questions

- What physical/emotional characteristics of the "illness" were presented?
- Did the "illness" affect any of the senses more than the others?
- Did the "illness" influence the personality of the character (Acne making the male defensive or ashamed, etc.)?
- Did the "illness" drive the plot?

Please be aware that players need to be sensitive in order to avoid making fun of people with illnesses or disabilities. Why not take a break from comedy and play this game seriously? You can find a helpful list in
Improv Ideas:
Film Titles — Page 61
Generic Scenes — Page 71

Type: Improv/Prepared
Skill: Intermediate
Group Size: 2
Equipment: None

We play this game because:

We want to see what effects illnesses may have on a character's physical and emotional state.

Emphasis:

Blocking and Conventions
Characterization
Concentration
Creativity
Ensemble Acting
Following Directions
Give and Take Focus
Group Dynamics
Listening and Silence
Memorization
Nonverbal Communication
Observation
Physical Control
Plot Structure
Spontaneity
Storytelling

Values

DEMO
10
MINUTES

PLAYER PREP
10
MINUTES

PERFORMANCE
2-3
MINUTES

Type: Prepared
Skill: Advanced
Group Size: 2
Equipment: Chairs, tables, stools

We play this game because:
Values help determine who we are as human beings.

Emphasis:

Blocking and Conventions
Characterization
Concentration
Creativity
Ensemble Acting
Following Directions
Give and Take Focus
Group Dynamics
Listening and Silence
Memorization
Nonverbal Communication
Observation
Physical Control
Plot Structure
Spontaneity
Storytelling

Discuss

What are values? How do they shape our personalities? Brainstorm a list of values (see Appendix, page 213 for more ideas).

Directions

- The group divides into pairs.
- Each pair is given two primary values and two secondary values.
- The director assigns a generic scene.
- Each pair gets ten minutes to plan a scene in which these values drive the personalities and choices of the characters.
- Scenes are presented to the class and the audience tries to determine what the values were and which values were primary and which were secondary.

Examples

The Car Accident:
Player A's values are family and speed. Player B's are creativity and sensibility. After the accident, A is frantic to get the rest of his family out of the car. He wants to do it immediately. Player B is frank that he doesn't think there is much hope, but, upon reflection, comes up with a creative way to rescue the family.

Focus Questions

- Were the values clear?
- Did the values shape the characters' personalities?
- Did the values contribute to the outcome of the plot?
- Was it clear which value was primary and which was secondary?

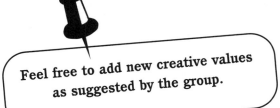

Feel free to add new creative values as suggested by the group.

You've Got a Secret

DEMO
0
MINUTES

PLAYER PREP
0
MINUTES

PERFORMANCE
5+
MINUTES

Directions

- Divide into teams of two. Teams divide into A's and B's.
- Player A is told a secret about player B and vice versa.
- A generic scene starts in which each player knows a secret about the other.
- The scene progresses as each player reacts to the other as if this secret is an important part of the other player.
- Players should eventually guess their own secrets.
- *Or,* players have secrets that affect their actions in the scene. The players try to guess each other's secret.

Focus Questions

- Did the players reveal the secrets by showing as opposed to telling?
- Did the players react to their endowments (secrets)?
- Did the secrets further the plot?

Type: Prepared
Skill: Intermediate/Advanced
Group Size: 2
Equipment: Furniture as needed

We play this game because:

Endowing a player with personality traits and having them guess helps improvisers to respond quickly and appropriately.

Emphasis:

Blocking and Conventions

Characterization

Concentration

Creativity

Ensemble Acting

Following Directions

Give and Take Focus

Group Dynamics

Listening and Silence

Memorization

Nonverbal Communication

Observation

Physical Control

Plot Structure

Spontaneity

Storytelling

Make sure the secrets are appropriate and not personal or hurtful.

Roommate

Type: Improv
Skill: Intermediate
Group Size: 2
Equipment: Benches or chairs

We play this game because:

Having roommates (or siblings) is a familiar situation for most.

Emphasis:

Blocking and Conventions
Characterization
Concentration
Creativity
Ensemble Acting
Following Directions
Give and Take Focus
Group Dynamics
Listening and Silence
Memorization
Nonverbal Communication
Observation
Physical Control
Plot Structure
Spontaneity
Storytelling

Discuss

Annoying habits of siblings.

Directions

- Two players come to the front of the group.
- While Player A leaves the room, the group tells Player B a terrible habit Player A has. (Example: never washes; keeps a pet rattlesnake; is messy; etc.) Player A returns, Player B leaves, and the group tells Player A a terrible habit Player B has. Player B returns. (Option: Each player may draw the habit of the other out of a hat.)
- When each roommate knows the other's bad habit, the scene begins.
- The object of the scene is for each player to play up the other's endowment and guess his own.

Focus Questions

- Were the endowments clearly hinted? (Show, don't tell.)
- How did the roommates hint at each other's endowments?
- How did the respective endowments determine the plot?
- How did the endowments contribute to the conflict?
- Were the conflicts resolved?
- How did the scene end?

The whole group can play this game in pairs with each player drawing a conflict. (See *Improv Ideas*, page 37) You can find a helpful list in *Improv Ideas*: Annoying Personal Habits — Page 17

Unit 18:
Exit, Stage Right! — Stage Directions

Lesson 41: Stage Directions and Awareness

Emphasis: Learning the basic stage areas and how to use them to create variety in scenes.

Equipment: Chair, stage areas map

Hint: After discussing the basic stage areas on the board, have players run through them and commit them to memory, as the body remembers best.

Solo Stage Directions   Minutes: 50-60
The more information the players are given, the more interesting the scene becomes.

Lesson 42: More Stage Directions

Emphasis: A re-emphasis of basic stage areas, this time with two players — each using different stage directions.

Equipment: Stage areas map

Hint: Before dividing into pairs, have the group as a whole imagine what two players could be doing given the stated stage directions.

Duo Stage Directions   Minutes: 50-60
Movement patterns (the given blocking in a script) can help determine the characters' emotions.

Solo Stage Directions

Type: Improv
Skill: Beginning/Intermediate
Group Size: 1
Equipment: Chair,
stage areas map

We play this game because:

The more information the player is given, the more interesting the scene can become.

Emphasis:

Blocking and Conventions

Characterization

Concentration

Creativity

Ensemble Acting

Following Directions

Give and Take Focus

Group Dynamics

Listening and Silence

Memorization

Nonverbal Communication

Observation

Physical Control

Plot Structure

Spontaneity

Storytelling

Directions

- Display and discuss a large diagram of the nine stage areas.
- Place a chair at Center Stage.
- The director chooses a volunteer to enter the playing area and gives the player a movement pattern. (Example: "Enter Up Left. Cross to Center and sit. Stand and cross Down Right. Cross Down Left. Exit Up Right.")
- After the player has walked through the pattern and seems to know it, the director gives the player an emotion.
- The player executes the movement pattern with that emotion.
- The director then adds a type of character. (Example: A happy kindergartener, a sad girlfriend.)
- The player executes the movement pattern with the emotion and the character.
- The director then adds a plot situation (Example: The happy kindergartener on the first day of school, the sad girlfriend getting a "Dear John" letter.)
- The player executes the pattern using the emotion, character, and situation.
- The player returns to the group, and another player is chosen to do the activity. Continue the activity until all players have performed or time runs out.
- Finally, the director reviews the stage areas with the group.

Focus Questions

- How much information was necessary for the player to really create a scene?
- How did the player motivate the movement from one stage area to the next?
- Were entrances and exits motivated?
- Did moving to the stage areas help the scene?
- Could the scene have been just as interesting if the player hadn't moved around so much?

See Appendix, page 212, for a stage areas map.

Duo Stage Directions

DEMO 10 MINUTES | PLAYER PREP 5 MINUTES | PERFORMANCE 45 MINUTES

Directions

- The director reviews the nine stage areas.
- Two volunteers (A and B) are chosen to act out a movement pattern. (Example: "A enters Upstage Left, crosses to Center, and sits. B enters Upstage Right, crosses to Center, and stands behind A. A crosses Downstage Left. B crosses Downstage Left, etc.)
- After A and B walk through the pattern, the group assigns characters to A and B. (Examples: A is an old lady; B is a robber. A is a big sister; B is an annoying little brother).
- The players then repeat the scene in character.
- Other elements (emotions, annoying habits, situations, genres, styles, time periods, types of weather, locations, etc.) are then added and A and B repeat the pattern, adding the new details.
- *Or,* the group is divided into many pairs, and each pair decides on a scenario, rehearses, and then performs in front of the entire group.

Focus Questions

- Did the given movement pattern determine the action of the scene?
- Did the types of characters given fit easily into the movement pattern?
- Did the types of characters work well together?

Challenge Players to Ramp It Up!

Assign status relationships (see *Improv Ideas* page 151) to characters to add conflict.

You can find a helpful list in *Improv Ideas*:
Attitudes — Page 11
Annoying Personal Habits — Page 17
Generic Scenes — Page 71
Genres — Page 73
Places — Pages 119-121
Weather — Page 169

Type: Improv/Prepared
Skill: Intermediate
Group Size: 2
Equipment: Stage areas map

We play this game because:

Movement patterns (the given blocking in a script) can help determine the emotions of the characters.

Emphasis:

Blocking and Conventions
Characterization
Concentration
Creativity
Ensemble Acting
Following Directions
Give and Take Focus
Group Dynamics
Listening and Silence
Memorization
Nonverbal Communication
Observation
Physical Control
Plot Structure
Spontaneity
Storytelling

Why Would You Do That?

Lesson 43: Beginning Motivation

Emphasis: Motivating action.

Equipment: None

Hint: Emphasize that most people's motivations and/or preferences for nonverbal communications are usually subtler than those used in improvisations.

Mixed Motivations　　　　　　　　　　　　**Minutes: 50-60**

When one performer wants one thing and the other wants something different, it automatically creates conflict!

Lesson 44: More Motivations

Emphasis: To show how conflicting desires may lead to conflict.

Equipment: None

Hint: Conflict may be small or large, but for beginning performers the more exaggerated the crisis the more obvious the problems will be.

We Don't See Eye-to-Eye　　　　　　　　**Minutes: 50-60**

Motivations/wants are essential elements of how characters carry the plot forward.

Mixed Motivations

DEMO
5
MINUTES

PLAYER PREP
10+
MINUTES

PERFORMANCE
2-3
MINUTES

Discuss

- How mixing motivations can lead to conflict.
- How some mixed motivations are too bland to create interesting conflicts (examples: to bore, to calm).
- How some mixed motivations are so volatile that the scenes can spiral out of control (example: to anger, to annoy).
- What are the implications for scene building and playwriting?

Directions

- Divide into teams of two.
- Two players draw or are assigned one motivation each.
- The group gives the players a generic situation.
- The players perform the scene emphasizing their motivations.

Examples

- A job interview in which the interviewer's motivation is to humiliate and the interviewee's motivation is to plead.
- A first date where the girl's motivation is to annoy and the boy's is to flatter.

Focus Questions

- Were the motivations clear?
- Did the motivations help us understand the characters?
- Did the motivations lead to conflict?
- Did the motivations lead to the scene's conclusion?

Challenge Players to Ramp It Up!

Perform *Mixed Motivations* as an improv with the audience offering a generic scene.

You can find a helpful list in *Improv Ideas*:
Generic Scenes — Page 71
Reasons/Wants/Motivations — Page 131

Type: Prepared
Skill: Intermediate
Group Size: 2
Equipment: None

We play this game because:

When one character wants one thing and the other wants something different, it automatically creates conflict.

Emphasis:

Blocking and Conventions
Characterization
Concentration
Creativity
Ensemble Acting
Following Directions
Give and Take Focus
Group Dynamics
Listening and Silence
Memorization
Nonverbal Communication
Observation
Physical Control
Plot Structure
Spontaneity
Storytelling

We Don't See Eye-to-Eye

DEMO
0
MINUTES

PLAYER PREP
2-3
MINUTES

PERFORMANCE
2-3
MINUTES

Type: Prepared
Skill: Intermediate/Advanced
Group Size: 2
Equipment: None

We play this game because:

Motivations/wants are essential elements of how characters carry the plot forward.

Emphasis:

Blocking and Conventions

Characterization

Concentration

Creativity

Ensemble Acting

Following Directions

Give and Take Focus

Group Dynamics

Listening and Silence

Memorization

Nonverbal Communication

Observation

Physical Control

Plot Structure

Spontaneity

Storytelling

Directions

- Divide into teams of two.
- Each player thinks of, draws, or is assigned a reason, want, or motivation.
- The audience may suggest a time and a place.
- The players have one to three minutes to act out a scene in which their reasons, wants, and/or motivations are in conflict.
- The scene must have a beginning, a middle, and an end. The scene must develop the conflict into a crisis and then resolve it.

Examples

- Players draw "to ace the test" and "to be popular," which suggests a nerd who is really smart and yet desperately wants to be accepted by the popular student who wants to cheat off his papers.
- Players draw "to cause trouble" and "to escape," which suggest a prison break where one prisoner is ready to make a break for it and his cellmate decides to blackmail him.

Focus Questions

- Were the motivations made clear?
- Did the motivations seem integral to the characters?
- How did varied motivations cause conflicts?
- Were the conflicts resolved?

You can find a helpful list in *Improv Ideas*:
Places — Pages 119-121
Reasons/Wants/Motivations — Page 131
Time Periods — Page 157

Thickening the Plot

Lesson 45: Plot Elements I

Emphasis: Building a plot with a clear beginning, middle, and end.

Equipment: None

Hint: It helps to discuss the concept of a "prompt" for scene building.

Tap In (Milwaukee Freeze Tag)   **Minutes: 30**
Body positions can often suggest character or action in an improvised scene.

Opening and Closing Scenes   **Minutes: 30**
It is often difficult to find beginnings or endings to scenes. These are good practice to learn how to motivate both.

Lesson 46: Plot Elements II

Emphasis: Adapting to changing plot scenarios.

Equipment: None

Hint: Since it's not easy to motivate drastic plot changes, emphasize that the suggested changes be logical.

What Comes Next?   **Minutes: 60**
Adapting to changing plot circumstances challenges players' abilities to motivate and carry the action forward.

Tap In (Milwaukee Freeze Tag)

Type: Improv
Skill: Beginning/Intermediate
Group Size: Whole group
Equipment: None

We play this game because:

Body positions can often suggest character or action in an improvised scene.

Emphasis:

Blocking and Conventions

Characterization

Concentration

Creativity

Ensemble Acting

Following Directions

Give and Take Focus

Group Dynamics

Listening and Silence

Memorization

Nonverbal Communication

Observation

Physical Control

Plot Structure

Spontaneity

Storytelling

Directions

- The players sit in a circle.
- Two volunteers start the game in the center of the circle.
- The audience suggests or the director assigns a starting place, time, situation, characters, line, etc.
- Starting with the prompt, the players create a scene with a beginning, middle, and end.
- When the players have established the plot and are in an interesting physical position, the director calls, "freeze." The actors "freeze" immediately.
- The director assigns a new player. The assigned player enters the circle and selects a player to replace.
- After studying the exact position of the actor to be replaced, the new player taps that player's shoulder. The replaced player leaves the middle of the circle, and the new player adopts the replaced player's position.
- The new player now starts a *new* improv based on the established physical relationship from the previous scene. In one line the new player gives the frozen actor enough information to participate.
- The process repeats until the director calls "freeze" again.

Focus Questions

- Did the players establish what and where they were right away?
- Did the players establish what they were doing?
- How did body positions determine the action of the scenes?

It is essential that the director maintains a quick pace.

Opening and Closing Scenes

DEMO **0** MINUTES	PLAYER PREP **0** MINUTES	PERFORMANCE **20+** MINUTES

Directions

(This game can be done as a solo or duet, silent or with dialog.)

- Divide into teams of two.
- Each pair is given, draws, or is assigned an opening or a closing scene.
- The players improvise the scene that takes place after the opening or before the closing scene.

Examples

- Opening Scene — "Enters, hears a noise, and jumps."
Player A enters furtively but jumps and hides when she hears player B enter. B enters as if it is his home and he is coming home from work. It soon becomes obvious that A has come to rob the house, not expecting B to come home.
- Closing Scene — "Looks around wildly and freezes."
A and B meet to plan a robbery. A is very apprehensive, and B convinces A that she can do it. This is A's first burglary, and she proceeds very cautiously through the window and into the house. Soon A relaxes and starts to pick up objects, putting them in a bag. The scene ends when an off-stage noise is heard and A looks around wildly, finally freezing with her hands in the air.

Focus Questions

- Were the preceding or proceeding scenes motivated by the assigned scene?
- Was the development logical/understandable?
- Was there a clear beginning, middle, and end?
- Did the character(s) have clear personalities which contributed to the motivated scenes?

Challenge Players to Ramp It Up!

- The players are given *both* an opening and a closing scene.
- Solo performers pantomime selected opening and closing scenes.

You can find a helpful list in *Improv Ideas*:
Opening and Closing Scenes — Page 109

Type: Improv/Prepared
Skill: Intermediate
Group Size: 1-2
Equipment: None

We play this game because:

It is often difficult to find beginnings or endings to scenes. These are good practice to learn how to motivate both.

Emphasis:

Blocking and Conventions
Characterization
Concentration
Creativity
Ensemble Acting
Following Directions
Give and Take Focus
Group Dynamics
Listening and Silence
Memorization
Nonverbal Communication
Observation
Physical Control
Plot Structure
Spontaneity
Storytelling

What Comes Next?

DEMO
0
MINUTES

PLAYER PREP
0
MINUTES

PERFORMANCE
5
MINUTES

Type: Improv
Skill: Intermediate/Advanced
Group Size: 2
Equipment: None

We play this game because:

This game emphasizes how complicated a plot can be and still have to make sense.

Emphasis:

Blocking and Conventions
Characterization
Concentration
Creativity
Ensemble Acting
Following Directions
Give and Take Focus
Group Dynamics
Listening and Silence
Memorization
Nonverbal Communication
Observation
Physical Control
Plot Structure
Spontaneity
Storytelling

Directions

- Two players come to the front of the room.
- They draw or are given a generic scene or a relationship (Examples: On a runaway train, siblings) and begin the scene.
- After about twenty seconds *or* when the players decide they are stuck and need a change, one of the players turns to the group and says, "What comes next?"
- Either the group or the director suggests a twist in the plot, and the scene continues.
- After another twenty seconds or so, the question is asked again, moving the scene in an extended direction.
- After about five minutes, the scene is concluded.

Examples

Brother and sister:
- A brother and sister are in a car going to the beach.
- A drunk driver hits them.
- The sister is injured.
- The brother tries to help her.
- The sister dies.

Teacher and student:
- A teacher and a student are discussing a test grade.
- The student becomes very angry.
- The teacher tears up the exam in exasperation.
- The student calms down, apologizes, and leaves.

Focus Questions

- Were the characters clearly depicted?
- Were the players able to creatively adapt to their changes?
- Did the changes make the scene more interesting?
- Were the players able to end the scenes on their own?
- Were the plot changes motivated?

At Odds

Lesson 47: Beginning Conflict

Emphasis: Developing a basic scene in an enclosed space.

Equipment: None

Hint: It is important to start this activity by discussing experiences group members have had in elevators.

Elevator   Minutes: 50

Being in a confined space can determine characters' actions. Confining the scene to a small space also makes it easier for performers to focus on the conflict rather than too many "where" details.

Lesson 48: Your Problem Is?

Emphasis: Building conflict by using a confined spaced.

Equipment: None

Hint: It's always interesting to start this session with stories from the participants about times they were trapped. Focus on how they felt at the time.

Trapped   Minutes: 50

Being trapped is in itself an emotional and a physical conflict.

At Odds (Continued)

Lesson 49: Playmaking with Conflict

Emphasis: Continuing to build suspense and conflict in scenes by setting a scene in a moving vehicle.

Equipment: Chairs, benches, classroom items

Hint: Before starting, brainstorm types of vehicles with the group. Then model how some of these can be suggested by use of simple classroom items (garbage can lids for wheels, stair units for levels, etc.). Stress that realism is not important.

Getting There Is Half the Fun   Minutes: 60
Being in a moving but confined space can help build physical tension.

Lesson 50: Conflict Games

Emphasis: Working with external and internal conflicts can be dramatic.

Equipment: One chair

Hint: This is a move from physical to situational conflict. Be sure to discuss the differences!

Standing, Sitting, Kneeling   Minutes: 20
Finding quick motivations for unusual body positions forces performers to adapt to new situations quickly.

Conflict Game   Minutes 40
Using ordinary life situations as conflicts can show how even these can be dramatic!

Elevator

DEMO **5** MINUTES PLAYER PREP **10** MINUTES PERFORMANCE **3** MINUTES

Directions

- Divide the players into groups of three.
- Each player in the group is a character in an elevator.
- Groups must plan a scene with a beginning, middle, and ending that takes place in the elevator. They must also plan a conflict that leads to the end of the scene.
- Groups present their scenes to the class.

Examples

- A lost child is on the elevator.
- The elevator breaks down.
- The elevator stops between floors.
- Someone exhibits claustrophobia as the doors close.

Focus Questions

- Did the scene have a beginning, a middle, and an ending?
- Did each of the players have a distinct character?
- Did the scene have a conflict?
- Did the conflict lead to the conclusion?

Type: Prepared
Skill: Beginning/Intermediate
Group Size: 3
Equipment: None

We play this game because:

So many dramas can and do happen in this small confined space that it provides many varied opportunities for improv.

Emphasis:

Blocking and Conventions
Characterization
Concentration
Creativity
Ensemble Acting
Following Directions
Give and Take Focus
Group Dynamics
Listening and Silence
Memorization
Nonverbal Communication
Observation
Physical Control
Plot Structure
Spontaneity
Storytelling

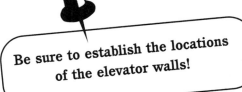

Be sure to establish the locations of the elevator walls!

Trapped

DEMO
3
MINUTES

PLAYER PREP
5
MINUTES

PERFORMANCE
3-5
MINUTES

Type: Prepared
Skill: Beginning/Intermediate
Group Size: 3-5
Equipment: None

We play this game because:

Being trapped is in itself an emotional and a physical conflict.

Emphasis:

Blocking and Conventions
Characterization
Concentration
Creativity
Ensemble Acting
Following Directions
Give and Take Focus
Group Dynamics
Listening and Silence
Memorization
Nonverbal Communication
Observation
Physical Control
Plot Structure
Spontaneity
Storytelling

Directions

- Divide players into groups of three to five.
- Players think of, draw, or are assigned an enclosed space.
- Players have five minutes to develop a one-minute scene in which one or more of the characters is trapped in the enclosed space. The scene must have a beginning, middle, and end.
- At the end, the situation of being trapped must be resolved in some way (rescue, escape, death, etc.).

Examples

Ferris Wheel: Three players, A, B, and C, ride the Ferris wheel. When it is time to get off, A and B get off quickly; the restraining bar snaps back down and C can't get out. C panics as he is hoisted into the air. It is no longer a fun ride. A and B watch — shouting advice and encouragement — as the wheel makes its circle. When the car comes to earth, A and B try to dislodge C. Finally C finds a small knob that releases the bar and comes back to earth triumphantly. The reunion is warm.

Focus Questions

- Could the audience tell where the players were?
- Was there a reason for the entrapment?
- Were the characters relevant to the plot?
- Were the characters well developed and unique?
- Did the scene have a beginning, a middle, and an end?
- Did the conflict have a resolution?

You can find a helpful list in *Improv Ideas*: Enclosed Spaces — Page 39

Getting There Is Half the Fun

DEMO
0
MINUTES

PLAYER PREP
10+
MINUTES

PERFORMANCE
3-5
MINUTES

Directions

- Each group chooses a vehicle to feature in the improv. The group may pantomime their vehicle or make it out of chairs, stools, and levels.
- The scene starts and ends in the vehicle. All action in the scene is prompted by what might happen in the vehicle.

Examples

- Limousine: A group of excited prom-goers have rented a limo to go to the prom. On the way to the dance the limo breaks down and the kids discover that the door locks are also jammed.
- City Bus: A man gets on a crowded bus with a suspicious-looking backpack. The riders all eye him and the backpack suspiciously as they are caught in traffic jam.

Focus Questions

- Was the vehicle clearly defined by the players?
- How did the players make the vehicle appear to move?
- Was being in the vehicle a springboard for the plot?
- Was being trapped the conflict or was it something more?
- Was the conflict resolved?
- Were the characters believable?
- Did the characters seem really trapped?
- Was there physical tension?

Type: Prepared
Skill: Beginning/Intermediate
Group Size: 4-5
Equipment: Benches, chairs, classroom items

We play this game because:

Being in a moving but confined space can help build physical tension.

Emphasis:

Blocking and Conventions
Characterization
Concentration
Creativity
Ensemble Acting
Following Directions
Give and Take Focus
Group Dynamics
Listening and Silence
Memorization
Nonverbal Communication
Observation
Physical Control
Plot Structure
Spontaneity
Storytelling

Creating an object with the players' bodies is very important in ensemble acting. You can find a helpful list in *Improv Ideas*: Vehicles — Page 163

Standing, Sitting, Kneeling

DEMO 5 MINUTES **PLAYER PREP 0 MINUTES** **PERFORMANCE 10+ MINUTES**

Type: Improv
Skill: Advanced
Group Size: 5
Equipment: One chair or stool

We play this game because:

Finding quick motivations for unusual body positions forces one to think divergently (outside the box).

Emphasis:

Blocking and Conventions
Characterization
Concentration
Creativity
Ensemble Acting
Following Directions
Give and Take Focus
Group Dynamics
Listening and Silence
Memorization
Nonverbal Communication
Observation
Physical Control
Plot Structure
Spontaneity
Storytelling

Directions

- One chair is placed in front of the group.
- Three players volunteer to play.
- One player sits in the chair. One player kneels. One player stands.
- A short practice scene is played using the initial positions.
- When the director indicates, the scene continues, but players can now move out of their initial positions.
- At all times one player needs to be seated, one standing, and one kneeling. When one player changes position, all players must adapt and motivate accordingly.

Focus Questions

- How difficult was it to be aware of the three positions?
- How difficult was it to motivate your new position?
- How did your position affect your character?
- How did the positions affect the plot?
- How difficult was it to keep moving and keep the scene going?
- How reliant were you on the others?

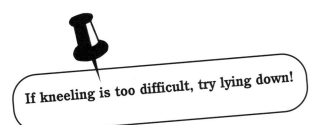

If kneeling is too difficult, try lying down!

Conflict Game

Discuss

What conflicts do the players experience in everyday life?

Directions

- Divide into teams of two. Players designate themselves A or B.
- Players draw or are assigned a dilemma.
- Players get three minutes to plan a three- to five-minute scene with a beginning (introducing characters and the beginning of a conflict), middle (acting out the conflict and adding small mini-conflicts or crises and/or a climax), and ending (resolution of the conflict and scene).

Focus Questions

- Were there clear characters?
- Were the characters' dilemmas clear?
- Did their conflicts lead to crises?
- Was the crisis clear?
- Was there a creative solution?
- Was the solution satisfying and conclusive?

Type: Prepared
Skill: Intermediate
Group Size: 2
Equipment: None

We play this game because:

Conflict and dramatic tension are the bases of all plots.

Emphasis:

Blocking and Conventions
Characterization
Concentration
Creativity
Ensemble Acting
Following Directions
Give and Take Focus
Group Dynamics
Listening and Silence
Memorization
Nonverbal Communication
Observation
Physical Control
Plot Structure
Spontaneity
Storytelling

It is important for players to understand that conflicts aren't necessarily arguments. You can find a helpful list in *Improv Ideas*: Dilemmas — Page 37

What a Character!

Lesson 51: Exaggeration in Characterization

Emphasis: Exaggerating personal characteristics helps create characters.

Equipment: None

Hint: Beginners have to exaggerate! Stress that this can be lots of fun and will generate a great many ideas. Do note, however, that this broad type of characterization usually has to be toned down in most stage plays.

If I Were a Skunk   **Minutes: 30**
Personification can add unusual depth to characterization.

The Wacky Family   **Minutes: 30**
Emotions can define groups as well as individuals, especially in forming mood.

Lesson 52: Internal Characterizations

May take 2 class periods

Emphasis: Understanding that what goes on internally affects character.

Equipment: List of generic situations, chairs, stools

Hint: Either one of these activities can — and may — take an entire class period!

Alter Egos   **Minutes: 30**
The use of alter egos can add depth to characterization or can be used as a comedy technique.

Time Out   **Minutes: 30**
Time out scenes can help add depth to characterization.

What a Character! (Continued)

Lesson 53: Characterization with Prompts

Emphasis: Using horoscopes and taking personality quizzes just for fun leads to high-interest prompts!

Equipment: Laminated cards with personality types

Hint: Before you play, discuss the personality stereotypes that are shown in daily horoscopes and magazine quizzes. See the appendix for horoscope signs and corresponding personality traits (page 214).

What's Your Sign?   Minutes: 50-60

Many people are interested in and influenced by horoscopes and personality quizzes. Using these to help externalize characterization can provide new insight.

Lesson 54: Characterization with Endowments

Emphasis: Playing more advanced games to extend the use of endowment in improv.

Equipment: Furniture

Hint: Keith Johnstone explains and uses endowments beautifully! Read *Impro* if you have time. Discuss endowments with the class before playing these games.

Stupid, Smelly, Sexy   Minutes: 30

Not all characters are perceived in the same way by each character with whom they interact. Mixing these up a bit can not only provide humor but also new insight into how to react to others' perceptions.

The Next-Door Neighbors   Minutes: 30

Annoying habits can help physicalize characterization.

If I Were a Skunk

DEMO **1** MINUTES
PLAYER PREP **0** MINUTES
PERFORMANCE **2-3** MINUTES

Type: Improv
Skill: Intermediate
Group Size: 2-6
Equipment: None

We play this game because:

Adding animal characteristics to humans can add interesting twists and/or depth to the character's physical portrayal and/or personality.

Emphasis:

Blocking and Conventions

Characterization

Concentration

Creativity

Ensemble Acting

Following Directions

Give and Take Focus

Group Dynamics

Listening and Silence

Memorization

Nonverbal Communication

Observation

Physical Control

Plot Structure

Spontaneity

Storytelling

Directions

- Choose one of the games in this book to play, and choose an appropriate number of players for the game.
- Each player thinks of, draws, or is assigned the name of an animal.
- In addition to following the other game directions, each player must *be* the selected animal in human form. The players may reveal their animals to the others in the scene.
- The audience guesses the animals at the end of the game/scene.

Examples

Make up a fictional title of a scene ("The Closet," "You Knew What I Would Do," "My Boyfriend Is an Alien," "The Sleepover," etc.).

Three players are chosen to act this scene — a cow, a coyote, and a rattlesnake. ("The Closet" — The characters are three siblings. The rattlesnake, who is the older brother, locks the cow in the closet. At first the silly coyote, who is the younger brother, goes along with it, but later he starts to regret it and tries to trick the snake into letting cow go.)

Focus Questions

- Did the players incorporate the physical qualities of the animals into the characterizations?
- Did the actors incorporate animal personalities (or stereotypes of)?
- Could you guess the animals? How?
- Did putting all these animals in one scene make sense?
- Did the plot incorporate the animals?

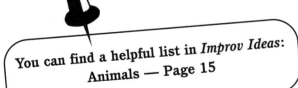

You can find a helpful list in *Improv Ideas*: Animals — Page 15

The Wacky Family

DEMO
0
MINUTES

PLAYER PREP
3-5
MINUTES

PERFORMANCE
2-3
MINUTES

Type: Prepared
Skill: Intermediate/Advanced
Group Size: 4-5
Equipment: None

We play this game because:

Emotions can define groups as well as individuals, especially in forming mood.

Emphasis:

Blocking and Conventions

Characterization

Concentration

Creativity

Ensemble Acting

Following Directions

Give and Take Focus

Group Dynamics

Listening and Silence

Memorization

Nonverbal Communication

Observation

Physical Control

Plot Structure

Spontaneity

Storytelling

Discuss

- How emotions can affect the mood of the entire group.

Directions

- Divide into teams of four to five players.
- Give the first team a scene title with a blank for an emotional adjective. (For example, if the scene is "blind date," the scene title will be "The _____ blind date.")
- The team draws an emotional adjective to fill in the blank. They have three minutes to plan (not rehearse) their scene.
- The team has up to three minutes to play a scene that uses their adjective to define the overall mood of the scene within the context of the title.
- Critique team one and repeat the process with the rest of the improv teams.

Examples

- The frightening SAT test.
- The sober visit to the doctor.
- The hysterical first day of school.

Focus Questions

- Did the actors each have a distinctive character with the overall mood?
- Did the emotion help determine the plot?
- Did the scene have a beginning, middle, and end?
- Did the title fit the scene?

Challenges Players to Ramp It Up!

- The scene starts immediately.
- Not all the characters have to have the emotion, but the adjective must be the main focus of the scene in order to act out the title.

Alter Egos

DEMO
0
MINUTES

PLAYER PREP
0
MINUTES

PERFORMANCE
2-3
MINUTES

Type: Improv
Skill: Beginning/Intermediate
Group Size: 4
Equipment: List of generic situations for director, chairs, stools

We play this game because:

The use of alter egos can add depth to characterization or can be used as a comedy technique.

Emphasis:

Blocking and Conventions

Characterization

Concentration

Creativity

Ensemble Acting

Following Directions

Give and Take Focus

Group Dynamics

Listening and Silence

Memorization

Nonverbal Communication

Observation

Physical Control

Plot Structure

Spontaneity

Storytelling

Directions

- Two volunteers are chosen to improvise.
- They come to the front of the group and are given a generic situation.
- The scene starts. After about thirty seconds, the director calls "freeze" and chooses two other players to be alter egos.
- The alter egos take their places behind the original players.
- The scene proceeds but after each original player speaks, his alter ego says what he really means.
- The original players proceed as if they do not know what the alter egos are saying.
- Each scene lasts two to three minutes.

Examples

- The first two players are a boy and a girl on a first date. As the scene proceeds they seem to really like each other. The alter egos reveal that they were forced to go out by their parents.
- The scene starts as a very typical job interview. As the alter egos get involved, it is revealed that the interviewer has no intention of hiring anyone for the position and the interviewee doesn't really want the job.

Focus Questions

- Did the alter egos create a believable alternative scenario?
- Did the presence of the alter egos disrupt the original scene?
- Did the presence of the alter egos add depth to the original characters?
- Did the alter egos distract?
- How could this technique be used in a play to enhance the script?

You can find a helpful list in *Improv Ideas*:
Generic Scenes — Page 71

Time Out

Directions

- Divide into groups of four or five.
- Each group is given a situation in which they might find themselves (see examples).
- Groups get ten to fifteen minutes to plan a scene in which the characters act out the scene with a beginning, middle, and an ending.
- During the course of the scene, each character must do at least one "time out" in which the scene freezes and the character steps out of the action and tells how he really feels.

Examples

- The Babysitter: A babysitter, her friend, and three little kids.
- The Family Reunion: Two parents, two kids, and a great-grandmother.
- The Birthday Party: The birthday child, two popular kids, and two outcasts.
- The School Dance: The principal, two parents, a boy, and a girl.

Focus Questions

- Was it difficult to freeze the action?
- Did the time outs add depth to the scene?
- Did the time outs help you understand the scene more completely?
- Did the time outs change the emotional quality of the scene?
- Were the time outs played for laughs? Did this help or hurt the scene?
- Did the time outs help players develop their characters?

Be sure to talk about the numerous TV shows that use the "Time Out" technique: *Clarissa Explains It All, Malcolm in the Middle, Saved by the Bell*, etc.

Type: Prepared
Skill: Intermediate/Advanced
Group Size: 4-5
Equipment: None

We play this game because:

Time out scenes can help add depth to characterization.

Emphasis:

Blocking and Conventions
Characterization
Concentration
Creativity
Ensemble Acting
Following Directions
Give and Take Focus
Group Dynamics
Listening and Silence
Memorization
Nonverbal Communication
Observation
Physical Control
Plot Structure
Spontaneity
Storytelling

What's Your Sign?

Type: Improv/Prepared
Skill: Intermediate/Advanced
Group Size: 2
Equipment: Laminated cards with personality types

We play this game because:

Horoscopes and personality quizzes influence many people. Using these to externalize characterization can provide new insights.

Emphasis:

Blocking and Conventions

Characterization

Concentration

Creativity

Ensemble Acting

Following Directions

Give and Take Focus

Group Dynamics

Listening and Silence

Memorization

Nonverbal Communication

Observation

Physical Control

Plot Structure

Spontaneity

Storytelling

Directions

- Each player receives a personality type (with or without a brief profile of the type).
- The group chooses a contemporary social issue.
- In pairs, the players improvise confronting the issue as their personality types.

Examples

- A helper and a completer grapple with the problem of teenage pregnancy.
- An Aries and a Virgo try to decide on a homework policy for the school.
- An introvert and an extrovert try to deal with the noise issue in their apartment building.

Focus Questions

- How did the different types confront the same problem?
- How did the different types present themselves physically? Emotionally?

Why not bring in the day's horoscopes from the local paper? Read them and use these "predictions" as prompts for improvs.

Stupid, Smelly, Sexy

DEMO 5 MINUTES

PLAYER PREP 0 MINUTES

PERFORMANCE 5 MINUTES

Directions

- Select four players. One player is the host of a gathering, and the other three players are guests.
- The players choose three attributes from a list of character traits (example: Attractive, stupid, and unkempt). Each player will secretly endow the other players with these three traits.
- The gathering begins as players enter one at a time.
- As players enter they try to act as they normally would at such a gathering, but they also subtly play their attitudes toward the others.
- The rest of the group observes for five minutes and the scene is frozen as they try to guess how each player feels about the others.

Example

- Player one is the host who thinks player two smells, player three is stupid, and player four is attractive. As a result she stays away from player two, is patronizing to player three, and tries to spend as much time as she can with player four.

Focus Questions

- How did each player interpret how to interact with the others' endowed traits?
- What happened when attitudes clashed?
- How was conflict created?
- How was conflict resolved?
- Was it possible to be reasonably subtle?

You can find a helpful list in *Improv Ideas*:
Character Traits — Pages 24-27

Type: Whole group
Skill: Advanced
Group Size: 4
Equipment: None

We play this game because:

Not all characters are perceived in the same way by the characters with whom they interact. Mixing these up not only provides humor, but also new insight into how to react to others' perceptions.

Emphasis:

Blocking and Conventions
Characterization
Concentration
Creativity
Ensemble Acting
Following Directions
Give and Take Focus
Group Dynamics
Listening and Silence
Memorization
Nonverbal Communication
Observation
Physical Control
Plot Structure
Spontaneity
Storytelling

The Next-Door Neighbors

Type: Prepared
Skill: Intermediate
Group Size: 3-5
Equipment: Furniture

We play this game because:

Annoying habits can help us physicalize characterization.

Emphasis:

Blocking and Conventions

Characterization

Concentration

Creativity

Ensemble Acting

Following Directions

Give and Take Focus

Group Dynamics

Listening and Silence

Memorization

Nonverbal Communication

Observation

Physical Control

Plot Structure

Spontaneity

Storytelling

Directions

- Divide into teams of three to five. Set up two simple houses on-stage.
- One player (the new neighbor) draws an annoying personal habit.
- The rest of the players create a scene that starts at their house (House 1) with the family discussing the new neighbor who has moved in next door (House 2).
- The new neighbor from House 2 visits the family in House 1.
- The family welcomes the new neighbor to their home. As the introductions continue, the new neighbor gradually exaggerates his annoying personal habit.

Examples

- The neighbor is a chronic gum chewer who tends to chew more quickly and loudly the more nervous she becomes.
- The neighbor talks too loudly, thus waking the neighbors' children.

Focus Questions

- How did the habit contribute to the personality of the neighbor?
- Did the habit remain constant or gradually build and recede?
- How did the neighbors manage to ignore the problem? Or did they?
- How did the habit further the plot? Did it lead to conflict? Was the conflict resolved?

Challenge Players to Ramp It Up!

There is more than one new neighbor and each of them has an annoying habit.

You can find a helpful list in *Improv Ideas*: Annoying Personal Habits — Page 17

Unit 23:
Fun with What We've Learned

Lesson 55: Combining Skills

May take 2 class periods

Emphasis: Combining three improv skills — endowment, focus, and motivation — to challenge players.

Equipment: Tables, stools, chairs

Hint: This game is one of the most popular improv games with middle school students. They can play it for hours at a time, enjoying the thrill of dramatic death scenes. Justine usually lets them have their fun and then discusses with them what they've learned about giving and taking focus, etc.

Death in a Restaurant   **Minutes: 50-60**

This game works on giving and taking focus, characterization, and motivation all in one game.

Lesson 56: Film Prompts

Emphasis: Enjoying improvisation inspired by film.

Equipment: Stools

Hint: Using imaginary plots for imaginary films stretches creativity levels.

Dubbing   **Minutes: 20-30**

Action and voice should go together in harmony.

Film Critics   **Minutes: 20-30**

Using directions from others to create improvised scenes leads to seeking information from scripts.

Fun with What We've Learned (Continued)

Lesson 57: Genres

Emphasis: Adapting genres in stories and theatre to improv.

Equipment: Furniture

Hint: Before you start, be sure to spend a fair amount of time defining the term "genre" and then giving well-known examples of various genres. Brainstorm with the class and list genres on the board if possible.

Genre House   Minutes: 50-60

Styles of films and television shows require different methods of acting — some stereotyped, others more realistic.

Lesson 58: Musical Genres

Emphasis: How musical styles can influence plot and character.

Equipment: None

Hint: Listen to songs from different musicals and music styles.

Musical Improv   Minutes: 50-60

Sometimes using musical variety frees the players to take new risks.

Death in a Restaurant

DEMO
5
MINUTES

PLAYER PREP
0
MINUTES

PERFORMANCE
10
MINUTES

Discuss

Before playing, talk about adventures the players may have had in restaurants.

Directions

- Divide into teams of six. Teams divide into three pairs of players. Pairs are numbered 1, 2, and 3.
- The players think of, draw, or are assigned a type of restaurant.
- Each pair chooses a relationship (e.g. mother/daughter, friends) and/or situation that may be the situation at the restaurant or before or after the meal (e.g. birthday celebration, prom, etc.).
- Each pair sits at a table (or stool) opposite each other.
- The director whispers "yes" or "no" to each player.
- The players who are told "yes" find a motivation for dying in the scene. They may *not* reveal this to anyone.
- The director calls a pair's number. That pair starts a conversation that reflects their relationship or situation.
- The director calls another pair's number. At this point the performing pair freezes exactly where they are, and the pair called starts a conversation.
- The director continues calling numbers at intervals with the performing pairs stopping *exactly* when another number is called and the called pair starting *precisely* where they left off.

Example

In a fast food restaurant there are three pairs of players: pair 1 is a mother and four-year-old son on an outing; pair 2 is a real estate agent and client; and pair 3 is a teenage couple eating before a movie. In pair 1, the little boy keeps choking on his French fries, but will he die? In pair 2 the client is irritating the real estate agent. In pair 3 both the boy and girl are wolfing down their food, obviously in a hurry. Who, if any, will die? And will the cause be obvious?

Focus Questions

- Did the players foreshadow their deaths or did they use red herrings (false clues)?
- Were there clear characters?
- Did the characters relate to each other?
- Was there status involved in the relationships?
- Were the groups able to freeze when necessary and pick up where they left off?
- Were the deaths motivated?

Type: Improv
Skill: Intermediate
Group Size: 6
Equipment: Tables, stools, chairs

We play this game because:

This game works on giving and taking focus, characterization, and motivation all in one game.

Emphasis:

Blocking and Conventions

Characterization

Concentration

Creativity

Ensemble Acting

Following Directions

Give and Take Focus

Group Dynamics

Listening and Silence

Memorization

Nonverbal Communication

Observation

Physical Control

Plot Structure

Spontaneity

Storytelling

You can find a helpful list in *Improv Ideas*: Restaurant Deaths — Page 133

Dubbing

DEMO
0
MINUTES

PLAYER PREP
0
MINUTES

PERFORMANCE
20+
MINUTES

Type: Improv
Skill: Beginning/Intermediate
Group Size: 4
Equipment: Stools

We play this game because:

Action and voice should go together in harmony.

Emphasis:

Blocking and Conventions
Characterization
Concentration
Creativity
Ensemble Acting
Following Directions
Give and Take Focus
Group Dynamics
Listening and Silence
Memorization
Nonverbal Communication
Observation
Physical Control
Plot Structure
Spontaneity
Storytelling

Directions

- Four players go to the front of the group.
- Two players are designated actors; two players are designated dubbers — one for each actor.
- The dubbers stand on the opposite side of the playing area from the actor they are dubbing.
- The group gives the actors a title or generic scene and the action starts.
- As the actors act silently, the dubbers provide the dialog.
- It should not be clear if the actors are following the dubbers or vice versa. It really doesn't matter.

Focus Questions

- How did the dubbing affect the acting?
- How did the acting affect the dubbing?
- Were the players able to develop a plot with a beginning, middle, and ending?
- Did the players often not know who was following whom?

It might be fun to show a scene from a badly dubbed foreign film.

Film Critics

DEMO 0 MINUTES · PLAYER PREP 0 MINUTES · PERFORMANCE 20+ MINUTES

Directions

- Divide into teams of five. Two players on the team are film critics. Three players act out the various films that the critics review.
- The critics think of, draw, or are assigned film titles.
- The critics comment on the films one at a time. They may identify a broad category (chick flicks, horror movies, worst films of the year) or discuss which films they like or dislike (thumbs up or thumbs down).
- As they establish commentary on the film, they identify a section of the film to be viewed ("Let's see the stunning climax," or "This is the moment when the lovers first meet.")
- The critics narrate the action as the three players act out the scene until the critics "stop" the film and either call for another scene from that film or go on to the next film.

Examples

"Today we review the five worst films of 2007! In fifth place we have the remake of *Night of the Living Dead, Part 11*. In this scene, the twins discover that their beloved granny has become a zombie. Let's see how they react in this typically stupid scene from the movie."

Focus Questions

- Was the information provided by the critics enough for the actors to develop their scenes?
- Did the actors capture the mood of the themes?

You can find a helpful list in *Improv Ideas*: Film Titles — Page 61

Type: Improv
Skill: Intermediate/Advanced
Group Size: 5
Equipment: Stools

We play this game because:

Using directions from others to create improvised scenes leads to seeking information from scripts.

Emphasis:

Blocking and Conventions
Characterization
Concentration
Creativity
Ensemble Acting
Following Directions
Give and Take Focus
Group Dynamics
Listening and Silence
Memorization
Nonverbal Communication
Observation
Physical Control
Plot Structure
Spontaneity
Storytelling

Genre House

DEMO
0
MINUTES

PLAYER PREP
0
MINUTES

PERFORMANCE
3-5
MINUTES

Type: Improv
Skill: Intermediate
Group Size: 2
Equipment: Assorted furniture, possible taped floor areas

We play this game because:

This high-energy game helps the players see how genres can affect emotional tone.

Emphasis:

Blocking and Conventions
Characterization
Concentration
Creativity
Ensemble Acting
Following Directions
Give and Take Focus
Group Dynamics
Listening and Silence
Memorization
Nonverbal Communication
Observation
Physical Control
Plot Structure
Spontaneity
Storytelling

Directions

- Divide into teams of two.
- Divide the playing area into four equal sections. The group decides what genre will be performed in each section.
- The group or director gives a title for the scene that reflects the starting genre. (Optional: The players are given a list of words from each genre that they may use to help their scene.)
- The players start a scene in the first genre, establishing who, when, and where.
- The director calls "switch," and the players move to a new area/genre and continue the scene in the new genre.

Example

Stage is divided into "children's," "news," "cooking," and "nature" genres. The title is *In the Cage*. The players start in the children's genre. One is the host, the other is the child. The host explains to the child that he has brought a very special animal to show her but that it has to be kept in the cage. The animal has yet to be revealed as they switch to the nature genre. In the nature area the host becomes the nature guide á la "The Crocodile Hunter," and explains how this fierce rattlesnake is about to be captured. The players move to the news genre as the host interviews a survivor of a rattlesnake bite and cautions residents to be on the lookout for snakes. The play ends in the cooking genre where two chefs prepare rattlesnake ragout.

Focus Questions

- Did the players establish characters that could adjust to the different genres?
- Were the transitions clear?
- Did the theme carry from genre to genre?
- Did the genres determine the tone?
- Were there mini-plots (with beginnings, middles, and endings) in each area?

You can find a helpful list in Improv Ideas:
Film Titles — Page 61
Clichés (and Tired Phrases) — Pages 29-31
Genres — Page 73

Musical Improv

DEMO	PLAYER PREP	PERFORMANCE
5 MINUTES	**0** MINUTES	**5** MINUTES

Directions

- Divide into teams of two.
- Divide the playing space into four areas. Each area represents a different song style.
- The audience suggests a scene title.
- The players start the scene in one area, eventually breaking into the song style of the area.
- They sing — in the appropriate style — in each performance area.

Examples

The Ocean Voyage: A couple starts in the romantic style singing about how they are going on a cruise for their honeymoon. They move though the lounge style as they sing about how cool it is to be on the ship. They then switch to the disco as they sing about the fun they're having socializing on board. Finally, they move to the hymn style as they realize the ship is sinking and they don't have much time left to live.

Focus Questions

- Did the styles immediately suggest plot ideas?
- Did the styles suggest characterizations?
- Once the basic plot and characters were introduced, was it easy to adapt them to each new song style?
- How did performing with music affect the mood of the scene?
- Were you able to incorporate dialog that led up to the song style?

Stress that it does *not* matter if the players sound good or match pitch. You can find a helpful list in *Improv Ideas*: Song Styles — Page 145

Type: Improv
Skill: Advanced
Group Size: 2
Equipment: Furniture as needed

We play this game because:

Sometimes using musical variety frees the players to take new risks.

Emphasis:

Blocking and Conventions
Characterization
Concentration
Creativity
Ensemble Acting
Following Directions
Give and Take Focus
Group Dynamics
Listening and Silence
Memorization
Nonverbal Communication
Observation
Physical Control
Plot Structure
Spontaneity
Storytelling

Doing It with Style

Lesson 59: Styles I

Emphasis: Using imaginary plots set in different times and styles.

Equipment: None

Hint: Before you start, be sure to start your session discussing various mannerisms, values, beliefs, and fashion styles in the different time periods. Brainstorm and put a list on the board.

In the Style Of   Minutes: 20-30
Different time periods can show that the same event can be interpreted very differently depending on the situation.

Past/Present/Future   Minutes: 30-40
The time period in which a scene is played determines much more than just the set.

Lesson 60: Styles II

Emphasis: Continuing work with different periods and styles to encourage quick, thoughtful changes in acting.

Equipment: Cards with time periods

Hint: Before starting, make sure to reinforce the perceived differences between the time periods you will be using.

Time Portal   Minutes: 50-60
Adapting quickly yet seamlessly to different staging requirements is an important acting skill.

In the Style Of

DEMO
0
MINUTES

PLAYER PREP
0
MINUTES

PERFORMANCE
3-5
MINUTES

Directions

- Divide into teams of two to four.
- The audience chooses a title or generic scene for the players to improvise.
- Players start the scene in the present (twenty-first century).
- As the scene progresses, the director calls out a new time period, and the players gradually shift to a new period and its requisite "style."

Focus Questions

- Were the players able to establish believable time periods?
- Were the transitions smooth?
- Were the plots logical for the time periods?
- Were there believable characters?

Challenge Players to Ramp It Up!

The entire group shows the same scene in different time periods.

It may help to show clips from TV shows or movies using different styles or time settings. You can find a helpful list in *Improv Ideas*: Time Periods — Page 157

Type: Improv
Skill: Advanced
Group Size: 3-5
Equipment: None

We play this game because:
Different time periods can show that the same event can be interpreted very differently depending on the situation.

Emphasis:

Blocking and Conventions

Characterization

Concentration

Creativity

Ensemble Acting

Following Directions

Give and Take Focus

Group Dynamics

Listening and Silence

Memorization

Nonverbal Communication

Observation

Physical Control

Plot Structure

Spontaneity

Storytelling

Past/Present/Future

DEMO
5
MINUTES

PLAYER PREP
5
MINUTES

PERFORMANCE
3-5
MINUTES

Type: Prepared/Improv
Skill: Intermediate/Advanced
Group Size: 4
Equipment: None

We play this game because:

The time period in which a scene is played determines much more than just the set.

Emphasis:

Blocking and Conventions

Characterization

Concentration

Creativity

Ensemble Acting

Following Directions

Give and Take Focus

Group Dynamics

Listening and Silence

Memorization

Nonverbal Communication

Observation

Physical Control

Plot Structure

Spontaneity

Storytelling

Directions

- Divide into teams of four.
- Choose a generic scene and a place suitable for time travel.
- The groups think of, draw, or are assigned a time in the past.

Game 1
The teams improvise the scene as it would be in the past, in the present, and in a future of their choosing.

Game 2
Have three teams, one showing the scene in the past, one showing the scene in the present, and one showing the scene in the future.

Game 3
Choose a historical moment and have different groups perform the generic scene in the time of that event. Perform the scenes chronologically.

Focus Questions

- How did the time period affect the plot?
- Did players physicalize their characters differently in the various time periods? Why or why not?
- Was the language used suitable to your idea of that time period?

Challenge Players to Ramp It Up!

As a class, make lists of "memory jogs" for past times (Roaring Twenties: short swingy skirts, women's short hair, bathtub gin, speakeasies, the Charleston, gangsters.)

Coordinate with history or literature classes to fit in with historical units in the curriculum. You can find a helpful list in *Improv Ideas*:

Generic Scenes — Page 71

Historical Moments — Page 87

Places — Pages 119-121

Time Periods — Page 157

Time Portal

DEMO
0
MINUTES

PLAYER PREP
1
MINUTES

PERFORMANCE
2-3
MINUTES

Directions

- Players divide into groups of three to five, and the playing area is divided in half.
- Players are given three cards with time periods on them and choose one to play.
- Players have one minute to decide how they will start the scene and how they will incorporate the time change on their chosen card.
- Play is started on one side of the stage, set in the present.
- When the director calls "switch" the players move to the other side (and time) of the stage and play the modified scene.
- The director calls "switch" again, and the players return to the present time to finish the scene.

Focus Questions

- In what ways did the time period affect the scene as it was played?
- In what way did the time change affect the anticipated resolution?
- Did the players choose to know about the time change ahead of time or let it happen spontaneously? Which do you think would be easier?
- Was the switch seamless?
- Could the audience tell what the new time was?

Challenge Players to Ramp It Up!

- A desk or chair is placed at the halfway mark of the playing area.
- Three cards, each with a time period on it, are placed face down on the desk or chair.
- Players start a scene suggested by the audience on one half of the stage.
- Once the scene is started the director calls "switch." The players take the top card from the desk/chair and pass to the other side of the stage (as if through a door), seamlessly moving their scene into the time period indicated.
- When the director calls "switch" again, they repeat the process, taking the next card, and moving into another time period.
- The director calls "switch" again and the scene is concluded in the final time period.

Type: Improv
Skill: Intermediate
Group Size: 3-5
Equipment: Cards marked with time periods

We play this game because:

Adapting quickly yet seamlessly to different staging requirements is an important acting skill.

Emphasis:

Blocking and Conventions
Characterization
Concentration
Creativity
Ensemble Acting
Following Directions
Give and Take Focus
Group Dynamics
Listening and Silence
Memorization
Nonverbal Communication
Observation
Physical Control
Plot Structure
Spontaneity
Storytelling

Creative Playmaking

Lesson 61: Playmaking with a Board Game

Emphasis: Introducing playmaking skills through the use of a board game.

Equipment: Spinergy®

Hint: It is important to bring in "props" every so often, and board games keep the interest high!

Spinergy®   Minutes: 50-60

Spin the three wheels to spark interesting word associations for playmaking!

Note: Spinergy® is great to play with its own directions, but it can also be adapted to a variety of improv situations. It calls for the same quick, abstract thinking as many improv games. Spinergy® is available through better book and toy stores. If you do not have access to Spinergy®, you may use other board games that call for interaction. Those games could include Tribong, Taboo, Therapy, Have I Got News for You, Scene It, Outburst, and Adversary.

Lesson 62: Playmaking with Flashback

Emphasis: Extending our repertoire of scene-building techniques by exploring the use of flashback.

Equipment: None

Hint: Before you start, discuss recent films/TV shows in which this technique was used and how effective it was.

Flashback   Minutes: 50-60

Knowing the background of a situation can give insight into why characters act they way they do.

Spinergy®

DEMO 5 MINUTES

PLAYER PREP 2-5 MINUTES

PERFORMANCE 3 MINUTES

Directions

- The director provides the game of Spinergy®, which consists of a cool random word generator with three word rings and a box of Scenario cards.
- The group is divided into groups of four.
- The director (or class member) spins the three wheels of the word generator to get three random words (example: neon, diaper, donut).
- The director chooses a Scenario card (example: Tell about the time you were saved by a platoon of Marines).
- Groups get two minutes to either act out a scene or tell a story responding to the Scenario card, using the three words.

Focus Questions

- Was it difficult to use the three words in your scene/story?
- In your group did a definite leader emerge?
- Did your scene/story make sense?
- Did the scenario help you to structure the relationships of the words?

Type: Improv
Skill: Beginning/Intermediate
Group Size: 4
Equipment: Spinergy®
a board game available from
GnuGames, Inc.

We play this game because:
Spin the three wheels to spark interesting word associations for playmaking!

Emphasis:

Blocking and Conventions
Characterization
Concentration
Creativity
Ensemble Acting
Following Directions
Give and Take Focus
Group Dynamics
Listening and Silence
Memorization
Nonverbal Communication
Observation
Physical Control
Plot Structure
Spontaneity
Storytelling

If you like Spinergy®, why not try other box games to inspire improvs? Check the appendix on page 199 for more games!

Flashback

DEMO
0
MINUTES

PLAYER PREP
10
MINUTES

PERFORMANCE
5
MINUTES

Type: Prepared
Skill: Intermediate/Advanced
Group Size: 5
Equipment: Furniture as needed

We play this game because:

Knowing the background of a situation can give insight into why characters act they way they do.

Emphasis:

Blocking and Conventions

Characterization

Concentration

Creativity

Ensemble Acting

Following Directions

Give and Take Focus

Group Dynamics

Listening and Silence

Memorization

Nonverbal Communication

Observation

Physical Control

Plot Structure

Spontaneity

Storytelling

Directions

- Divide into groups of four.
- Give each group a generic scene or title.
- Groups prepare scenes around the given title. Scenes are to include at least two flashback scenes illustrating events that may have led up to or contributed to the present scene.

Examples

- The Blind Date: A boy and a girl have been set up by their parents to go to a school dance. They are at the dance having a horrible time.
- Flashback 1: The parents, who are good friends, have dinner together and discuss how their children would just love each other and should meet.
- Flashback 2: At school the girl discusses what a geek the boy is and how she's glad she doesn't have to spend time with him even though her parents are friends with his parents.
- The Audition: A girl is auditioning for a part in the school musical run by a very critical director.
- Flashback 1: The girl's friends dare her to audition.
- Flashback 2: The girl's mother goes on and on about how she had the lead in her school musical when she was the girl's age.

Focus Questions

- Did the scene have a beginning, middle, and ending?
- Did the flashbacks add depth to the scene?
- Were the flashbacks necessary to understanding the scene?
- Did the flashbacks add to the conflict?

Challenge Players to Ramp It Up!

- Do a flash forward.
- Use these ideas for longer, more involved playmaking.
- Discuss how these scenes could be incorporated into a full-length play.

Well-Known Stories at Work

Lesson 63: Spoofs

Emphasis: Spoofing well-known stories.

Equipment: None

Hint: It is important to learn to use and understand satire, spoof, and parody, as these are major players in today's comedy. Start the session discussing various known spoofs (*Blazing Saddles, Young Frankenstein, Austin Powers*, etc.) and then discuss how well-known tales could be "twisted" in order to spoof them.

Fractured Fairy Tales   Minutes: 50-60
Twisting well-known fairy tales and myths can be played for comedy or drama. No matter which you choose, new insights will be gained, making these timeless tales even richer.

Lesson 64: Point of View

Emphasis: Interpreting well-known stories by observing very different takes on the same situation.

Equipment: None

Hint: Seeing the same situation through various characters' eyes enriches the dimensions of any plot.

It's All in the Point of View   Minutes: 50-60
In any story there are many points of view on which to focus.

Fractured Fairy Tales

Type: Prepared
Skill: Intermediate/Advanced
Group Size: 4-5
Equipment: None

We play this game because:

Sometimes a twist on an established plot can add depth and/or humor to an old "war horse."

Emphasis:

Blocking and Conventions

Characterization

Concentration

Creativity

Ensemble Acting

Following Directions

Give and Take Focus

Group Dynamics

Listening and Silence

Memorization

Nonverbal Communication

Observation

Physical Control

Plot Structure

Spontaneity

Storytelling

Directions

- Divide into groups of four to five.
- A member of each group thinks of, draws, or is assigned a title of a well-known fairy tale.
- Each group gets five to ten minutes to develop a slightly fractured version of the tale.
- The group performs the new version in approximately five minutes. Versions may be funny or serious.

Examples

- *The Three Billy Goats Gruff* set on and under a bridge where homeless people sleep.
- *The Emperor's New Clothes* set during New York Fashion Week.
- *The Frog Prince* set at the high school prom.

Focus Questions

- Was the plot recognizable?
- Were there modified characters?
- Did the new version add a new dimension to the old plot?
- Was there clear development and a beginning, middle, and end?

Try setting tales in different time periods! You can find a helpful list in *Improv ideas*: Fairy, Folk, and Children's Stories — Page 51

It's All in the Point of View

DEMO
0
MINUTES

PLAYER PREP
15+
MINUTES

PERFORMANCE
5
MINUTES

Directions

- Players divide into groups of four to five.
- Players choose a favorite fairy tale.
- Players choose three characters from this fairy tale and perform three short scenes, showing the plot from each character's point of view.
- The scenes may be in story format or courtroom scenes, deathbed confessions, jail interviews, etc.

Examples

- *The Three Little Pigs* from the point of view of the wolf, the third little pig, and the neighborhood social worker.
- *Cinderella* from the point of view of the Fairy Godmother, Cinderella's father, and one of the stepsisters.
- *Hansel and Gretel* from the point of view of the Witch, the stepmother, and Gretel.

Focus Questions

- Were there three distinct points of view in the stories?
- Were the points of view clear?
- Did the characters change personalities as seen from others' points of view?
- Were conflicts resolved in different ways depending on the point of view?

Variations

- Switch the point of view at various points within one longer scene.

You can find a helpful list in
Improv ideas:
Fairy, Folk, and Children's Stories — Page 51

Type: Prepared
Skill: Advanced
Group Size: 4-5
Equipment: None

We play this game because:
In any story there are many points of view on which to focus.

Emphasis:

Blocking and Conventions
Characterization
Concentration
Creativity
Ensemble Acting
Following Directions
Give and Take Focus
Group Dynamics
Listening and Silence
Memorization
Nonverbal Communication
Observation
Physical Control
Plot Structure
Spontaneity
Storytelling

The Plot Thickens

Lesson 65: Plot It Yourself

Emphasis: Mixing and matching plot, character, and location to create developed improvs.

Equipment: Cards: Group 1 with subjects (who); Group 2 with predicates (what/action); Group 3 with locations (where)

Hint: Use the *Official Movie Plot Generator* (see Appendix, page 220) if you have a copy, and go through several possible scenarios before starting.

Mix and Match   **Minutes: 50-60**

Adapting quickly to new information, logical or not, is an essential part of improvisation.

Lesson 66: Plot Organization

Emphasis: Creatively solving a problem through plot developments.

Equipment: None

Hint: Developing a plot chronologically makes the process clearer as it provides a built-in beginning, middle, and ending structure.

The Invention Of   **Minutes: 50-60**

Inventing a product is similar to structuring a plot.

Mix and Match

DEMO
0
MINUTES

PLAYER PREP
10
MINUTES

PERFORMANCE
2-3
MINUTES

Directions

- Groups divide into small groups of four.
- Each group draws three cards: one with a subject, one with a predicate, and one with a location (see examples).
- Using the three who, what, and where cards, players put together a two- to three-minute scene to be performed for the other groups.

Examples

- Hockey players; sing; closet: A group of rowdy hockey players sing Christmas carols in a dark closet.
- Encyclopedia salesmen; record; South America: A convention of encyclopedia salesmen records a hit rap song in South America.
- Children; win lottery; downtown New York City: A classroom of nursery school children wins the lottery in downtown New York City.

Focus Questions

- How did you motivate seemingly mismatched who, what, and where cards to make sense?
- Was it difficult to create a beginning, a middle, and an ending?
- Did some of the mismatches create interesting plots?

Challenge Players to Ramp It Up!

- Play *Mix and Match* as an improv.

Type: Prepared
Skill: Intermediate/Advanced
Group Size: 4
Equipment: Cards: Group 1 with subjects (who); Group 2 with predicates (what/action); Group 3 with locations (where)

We play this game because:
Adapting quickly to new information, logical or not, is an essential part of improvisation.

Emphasis:

Blocking and Conventions
Characterization
Concentration
Creativity
Ensemble Acting
Following Directions
Give and Take Focus
Group Dynamics
Listening and Silence
Memorization
Nonverbal Communication
Observation
Physical Control
Plot Structure
Spontaneity
Storytelling

DEMO
0 MINUTES

PLAYER PREP
3 MINUTES

PERFORMANCE
3-5 MINUTES

Type: Prepared
Skill: Intermediate/Advanced
Group Size: 3-4
Equipment: None

We play this game because:
Inventing a product is similar to structuring a plot.

Emphasis:

Blocking and Conventions

Characterization

Concentration

Creativity

Ensemble Acting

Following Directions

Give and Take Focus

Group Dynamics

Listening and Silence

Memorization

Nonverbal Communication

Observation

Physical Control

Plot Structure

Spontaneity

Storytelling

Directions
- Divide into groups of three to four.
- Audience members call out the name of an unusual product, real or imaginary.
- The players take three minutes to plan a three- to five-minute documentary scene showing how this product came to be invented.

Examples
- The product may come from a well-known historical event (the egg beater in the Chinese earthquake).
- The product may be a fantasy event (dragons inventing fire balls).
- The product may be an offshoot of an existing product (how mixing bowls became helmets for soldiers in WWII).
- The product itself may be something unheard of, and the scene can show not only its invention, but its use.

Focus Questions
- Did the players each have a distinctive character in the scene?
- Did the scene show a logical progression?
- Was there a moment when the characters discovered how to invent the product?
- Was the technique creative?

Challenge Players to Ramp It Up!
The players immediately improvise the documentary scene.

You can find a helpful list in *Improv Ideas*: Cool and Unusual Products — Page 35

Prompts, Please

Lesson 67: Prompts

Emphasis: Playing basic games and creating a nontraditional news broadcast.

Equipment: Newspapers

Hint: Everyone reads or glances at a newspaper, and most people are aware of the daily news broadcasts. Discuss variety before playing.

Newsies (See page 27)   Minutes: 10-15
Sometimes it is freeing to express yourself emotionally when you are not being directly observed.

Anchorman   Minutes: 40-50
Interpreting unusual headlines without knowing the story behind them can lead to creativity.

Lesson 68: Scenes from Prompts

Emphasis: Prompting scenes with fortunes from fortune cookies.

Equipment: Tables and chairs, fortunes from fortune cookies

Hint: To engage the group, bring in real fortune cookies and break some open.

Today's Your Lucky Day   Minutes: 50-60
These can be set in a restaurant or used alone for plot inspiration.

Anchorman

DEMO
0
MINUTES

PLAYER PREP
15+
MINUTES

PERFORMANCE
5+
MINUTES

Type: Prepared
Skill: Intermediate/Advanced
Group Size: 4
Equipment: Newspaper
headlines

We play this game because:

Interpreting unusual headlines without knowing the story behind them can lead to creativity.

Emphasis:

Blocking and Conventions
Characterization
Concentration
Creativity
Ensemble Acting
Following Directions
Give and Take Focus
Group Dynamics
Listening and Silence
Memorization
Nonverbal Communication
Observation
Physical Control
Plot Structure
Spontaneity
Storytelling

Directions

- Players are divided into groups of four.
- Groups draw four or five headlines each. (Headlines can be taken from standard newspapers or, our favorite, the *Weekly World News*!)
- Groups get fifteen to twenty minutes to plan a news broadcast using only these headlines.
- Characters are interchangeable. Suggested characters are anchorpersons, reporters, interviewers, and participants in the news items.
- News broadcasts are presented to the class.

Focus Questions

- Were the formats used interesting and involving?
- Was there variety, or were the items static?
- Were the interpretations of the headlines creative?
- Did the broadcast have a beginning, a middle, and an ending?
- Did the individual headlines have a beginning, a middle, and an ending?

Have the group start collecting interesting headlines a few days before the activity. You can find a helpful list in *Improv Ideas*: News Commentary Ideas — Page 85

Today's Your Lucky Day

DEMO **3** MINUTES   PLAYER PREP **0** MINUTES   PERFORMANCE **5** MINUTES

Directions

- Divide into teams of four. Set up a table at a Chinese restaurant in the playing area.
- The players start the scene as diners at the end of the meal.
- The director gives one of the players a "fortune cookie" (a slip of paper or index card with a fortune).
- The player with the fortune reads the fortune to the other players, and the scene progresses incorporating the fortune.

Examples

- "Don't drink that!" The waiter brings all the customers cups of after-dinner coffee along with the bill. One of the players reads his fortune as they all hear a scream from the other table — a customer has discovered that the coffee is so hot that he has burned himself.
- "You will discover the meaning of life." As the customer reads his fortune out loud, his wife blushes and tells him that she is going to have a baby — an event that the poor couple never thought would be possible.

Focus Questions

- How difficult was it for the players to incorporate the fortune into the scene?
- Did the fortune further the plot?
- Did the scene make sense?
- Was there a conclusive, logical ending to the scene?

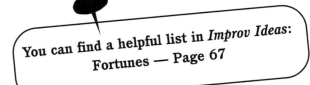

You can find a helpful list in *Improv Ideas*: Fortunes — Page 67

Type: Improv
Skill: Advanced
Group Size: 4
Equipment: Tables and chairs as needed, optional: fortunes from fortune cookies

We play this game because:
Everyone knows and loves the fortunes in fortune cookies. They make great props.

Emphasis:

Blocking and Conventions
Characterization
Concentration
Creativity
Ensemble Acting
Following Directions
Give and Take Focus
Group Dynamics
Listening and Silence
Memorization
Nonverbal Communication
Observation
Physical Control
Plot Structure
Spontaneity
Storytelling

Challenges

Lesson 69: Character Exaggeration

Emphasis: Including superheroes and villains to enhance plots.

Equipment: List of villains

Hint: We often see the world in terms of extremes: black/white, good/bad, strong/weak. In fact, a great deal of comedy comes from the exaggeration of these traits. It's fun to play with these for a break.

To the Rescue   Minutes: 20-30
Exaggeration of characters can add interesting insights into characterization and/or be played for comedy.

Bad Guy/Good Guy   Minutes: 20-30
Bad guys are often the most interesting of characters to play because their personalities are often so exaggerated.

Lesson 70: Ensemble Acting

May take 2 class periods

Emphasis: Working with body positions, accents, and attitudes to enhance plot and character

Equipment: Chairs, benches, a fake steering wheel

Hint: Working together as a unit is imperative to improv as well as acting. These fast-paced but fun games reinforce this skill.

Stop and Go   Minutes: 20
Changing quickly from one scene to the next is an important improv skill.

Hitchhiker   Minutes: 30-40
This high-energy game can last an entire period or be used as a warm-up!

To the Rescue

DEMO	PLAYER PREP	PERFORMANCE
3 MINUTES	**5+** MINUTES	**2-3** MINUTES

Directions

- The group thinks of a serious crisis (example — a tidal wave about to hit the city).
- Two players are endowed with "super powers" (example — News Broadcaster Lady and Urge to Scream Guy).
- The two players play the scene trying to use their "super powers" to avert the crisis.

Examples

- Ballet Lady leaps over a burning building and tosses a baby to Jumping Jack Guy.

Focus Questions

- Did the players act out their super powers?
- Did the super powers solve the crisis?
- Did the superheroes interact with each other in a superhero sort of way?
- Did the powers help save the day?

Discuss famous superheroes/crime fighters and how their special powers are used to fight crime. Watch the scene in *The Incredibles* that shows the defeated superheroes. You can find a helpful list in *Improv Ideas*:
Superheroes — Page 153

Type: Prepared
Skill: Intermediate/Advanced
Group Size: 2
Equipment: None

We play this game because:

Exaggeration of characters can add interesting insights into characterization and/or be played for comedy.

Emphasis:

Blocking and Conventions
Characterization
Concentration
Creativity
Ensemble Acting
Following Directions
Give and Take Focus
Group Dynamics
Listening and Silence
Memorization
Nonverbal Communication
Observation
Physical Control
Plot Structure
Spontaneity
Storytelling

Bad Guy/Good Guy

DEMO
0
MINUTES

PLAYER PREP
5+
MINUTES

PERFORMANCE
2-3
MINUTES

Type: Prepared
Skill: Intermediate/Advanced
Group Size: 2
Equipment: List of villains

We play this game because:

Bad guys are often the most interesting of characters to play because their personalities are often so exaggerated.

Emphasis:

Blocking and Conventions

Characterization

Concentration

Creativity

Ensemble Acting

Following Directions

Give and Take Focus

Group Dynamics

Listening and Silence

Memorization

Nonverbal Communication

Observation

Physical Control

Plot Structure

Spontaneity

Storytelling

Directions

- Divide group into pairs where one player is A and the other is B.
- A draws the name of a super villain.
- A and B perform a scene in which the super villain causes a crisis for B.

Examples

- A is Jafar (from *Aladdin*). B is a soldier in Iraq. A tricks B into walking into a trap and getting captured.
- A is a *Opera Singer*. B is A's date. A tries to convince B to stay out after curfew by singing snatches of the new opera she is in.

Focus Questions

- Did the type of villain help determine the plot?
- Did the villain create the crisis?
- Did the scene end in a disaster, or did B overcome the villain's treachery?

Bring in pictures of different characters and ask the group which they think are good guys and which are bad guys. You can find a helpful list in *Improv Ideas*: Super Villains — Page 155

Stop and Go

DEMO
0
MINUTES

PLAYER PREP
0
MINUTES

PERFORMANCE
15+
MINUTES

Directions

- Choose three volunteers to play and three volunteers to sculpt.
- Players go to the front of the group where they are "sculpted" into a picture by the three sculptors. When the sculptors finish they call "freeze."
- The three players get a chance to take in the freeze for a moment.
- When the director says "Go!" the players must create a scene. (They move out of their frozen state which is only used as a beginning point for the scene.)
- After twenty to thirty seconds the director calls "Stop," and the players freeze exactly where they are.
- A few seconds later the director calls "Go!" and a new scene begins.
- The game continues as before, ending after the three players have created ten to fifteen different scenes.

Focus Questions

- Did moving around help the players create the new scenes?
- Did using levels help?
- Did scenes seem to flow into each other?
- Was it difficult to think of new scenes?
- Did a leader emerge?
- Did one person seem to be excluded?

Type: Improv
Skill: Intermediate/Advanced
Group Size: 6
Equipment: Chairs, benches, step units, etc.

We play this game because:

Changing quickly from one scene to the next is an important improv skill.

Emphasis:

Blocking and Conventions

Characterization

Concentration

Creativity

Ensemble Acting

Following Directions

Give and Take Focus

Group Dynamics

Listening and Silence

Memorization

Nonverbal Communication

Observation

Physical Control

Plot Structure

Spontaneity

Storytelling

Hitchhiker

DEMO
0
MINUTES

PLAYER PREP
0
MINUTES

PERFORMANCE
2-3
MINUTES

Type: Improv
Skill: Intermediate
Group Size: 5
Equipment: 2 benches or 5-6 chairs; a fake steering wheel is also fun (any kind of flat circular object will do)

We play this game because:

This is a high-energy game that can last an entire period or be used as a warm-up!

Emphasis:

Blocking and Conventions
Characterization
Concentration
Creativity
Ensemble Acting
Following Directions
Give and Take Focus
Group Dynamics
Listening and Silence
Memorization
Nonverbal Communication
Observation
Physical Control
Plot Structure
Spontaneity
Storytelling

Directions

- Divide into teams of five. Set up a "car" with two chairs in front and three in back.
- The first player serves as the driver and sits in the car. The rest of the players each think of, draw, or are assigned an accent or an attitude.
- One at a time the players enter the scene as hitchhikers. When they enter the car, each has a clear accent or attitude.
- As soon as each new hitchhiker enters the car, everyone in the car assumes the new player's accent or attitude.
- The exercise is over when all the hitchhikers have entered and changed the scene. The driver finds a motivation to end the scene.

Example

The driver has established that she is on her way to a shopping mall. Hitchhiker 1 is picked up and establishes that he is from the south. Driver is interested, as her grandmother was also from that area of the country. They chat about southern cooking until they pick up Hitchhiker 2 from Italy. Conversation changes to pasta. They pick up Hitchhiker 3, who is from England. The conversation changes to a discussion on Anglo-American relations. Hitchhiker 4 is from France, and conversation focuses on fashion opportunities at the stores in the mall. Hitchhiker 5 comes last. Being that he is Jamaican, they all decide to abandon their shopping plans and go dancing at a club.

Focus Questions

- Was it easy to assume the new hitchhiker's accent or attitude?
- How did this change the plot?
- Was the conclusion motivated?

You can find a helpful list in *Improv Ideas*: Accents and Attitudes — Page 11

Unit 30:
The Tension Mounts —
Suspense and Storytelling

Lesson 71: Scenes with Suspense I

Emphasis: Setting the scene for suspense with a favorite party game.

Equipment: None

Hint: *Murder in the Dark* is actually an ensemble activity, but we place it here because it moves us into thinking of crime and suspense.

Murder in the Dark   **Minutes: 50-60**

Actors must be aware of even the most minute hints about who, what, when, where, and while.

Lesson 72: Scenes with Suspense II

May take 2 class periods

Emphasis: Creating a complete scene with a definite conflict.

Equipment: Lists of rooms, crimes, and weapons

Hint: In the twentieth century we called this "Sherlock Holmes." It combines playmaking skills with plot, character, and location. (Who, what, and where!)

CSI: Your Hometown   **Minutes: 50-60**

It integrates the who, what, and where in the well known "crime-solving" format.

The Tension Mounts —
Suspense and Storytelling (Continued)

Lesson 73: Storytelling

Emphasis: Creating basic stories.

Equipment: Chairs

Hint: The process of building a story can be free and spontaneous. After stories have been created, discuss the elements of a story.

First Line/Last Line (see page 83)   Minutes: 20-30
Learning to motivate actions and lines is a first step in becoming an actor.

Word Association   Minutes: 20-30
Sometimes creativity demands that we bypass "logic" and come up with unusual associations.

Lesson 74: Storytelling with Suspense

Emphasis: Using only voices to create suspenseful stories.

Equipment: Noisemakers, lists of situations, a table

Hint: Before starting the games, discuss films/TV shows that use sound to create suspense. Show recorded examples and then play the same video or DVD without sound.

This Sounds Like the Place   Minutes: 15-20
Understanding how sounds can go together to create environments is essential.

Suspense   Minutes: 30-40
Background sounds can greatly enhance a scene.

Murder in the Dark

DEMO 0 MINUTES

PLAYER PREP 0 MINUTES

PERFORMANCE 50+ MINUTES

Directions

- The group spreads out around the room.
- All players close their eyes and move slowly around the room.
- The director circulates and taps one player firmly on the shoulder. This player is "the murderer."
- The murderer then circulates with his eyes open and lightly taps a victim on the head.
- When tapped, the victim counts to five while moving and then screams and falls to the ground.
- The group then freezes, everyone opens their eyes, and the director gives the group three guesses as to the identity of the murderer.
- If the murderer is guessed, a new murderer will be selected in the same way.
- If the murderer is not guessed, then the murderer remains the same and the play continues.

Focus Questions

- How was the murderer guessed?
- What did the murderer do to trick the group?

Type: Whole group
Skill: Beginning
Group Size: Whole group
Equipment: None

We play this game because:

Actors must be aware of even the most minute hints about who, what, when, where, and while.

Emphasis:

Blocking and Conventions

Characterization

Concentration

Creativity

Ensemble Acting

Following Directions

Give and Take Focus

Group Dynamics

Listening and Silence

Memorization

Nonverbal Communication

Observation

Physical Control

Plot Structure

Spontaneity

Storytelling

CSI: Your Hometown

DEMO
0
MINUTES

PLAYER PREP
10
MINUTES

PERFORMANCE
5
MINUTES

Type: Prepared
Skill: Advanced
Group Size: 4-6
Equipment: Lists, chairs, stools, levels, props as needed

We play this game because:

It integrates the who, what, and where in the well known "crime-solving" format.

Emphasis:

Blocking and Conventions

Characterization

Concentration

Creativity

Ensemble Acting

Following Directions

Give and Take Focus

Group Dynamics

Listening and Silence

Memorization

Nonverbal Communication

Observation

Physical Control

Plot Structure

Spontaneity

Storytelling

Directions

- Divide into groups of four to six. Each group draws a room, a crime or imaginary crime, and a weapon.
- Given these three starters, each group develops a scene about their crime. The scene may show the crime, the aftermath of the crime, or a detective discovering and solving the crime.
- Scenes should be about five minutes long and should have a complete plot with a beginning, middle, and an ending.

Examples

- "An abduction in the attic with an abandoned refrigerator." The scene starts as someone in the family realizes that their little girl is missing. The search eventually moves to the attic where the child is discovered, alive, locked inside an old fridge stored in the attic.
- "Blackmail in the corridor with a scorpion." In the corridor of a bio-science laboratory, a research scientist corners one of the company's directors. The scientist holds a deadly scorpion in a jar and threatens to kill the director unless he stops doing research on cloning.

Focus Questions

- Were the three elements of crime, weapon, and room able to determine a plot?
- Did the plot suggest vivid characters?
- Was the plot clearly developed?
- Did the scene have a clear focus?
- Did the scene have a definite conclusion?
- Could this scene be part of a larger narrative?

Just for fun, play the board game of *Clue* or view the film. You can find a helpful list in *Improv Ideas*:
Rooms in a House — Page 135
Crimes — Page 136
Murder Weapons — Page 137

Word Association

DEMO
0
MINUTES

PLAYER PREP
0
MINUTES

PERFORMANCE
20+
MINUTES

Directions

- The group sits in a circle. The director asks for a suggestion of a word on which to make an association (snow, dinosaur, SUV, movie star, etc.).
- Starting with that word, the next player associates on that word (see example).
- The next player in the circle associates the previous word, *not* the first word. Play continues until every player has made an association.
- Take two words — the first and the last — and ask for volunteers to make up a brief story using those two words.
- After the story, a new word is chosen and the play starts again.

Examples

- SNOW – rain – sleet – slippery – fall – spring – jump – rope – hang – execution – MURDERER.
- SUV – big – little – leprechaun – Ireland – green – blue – sad – happy – SMILE.

Story Ideas

- Snow – Murderer. A murderer ties to escape the scene of the crime but slips on ice hidden under the snow.
- SUV – Smile. A husband surprises his wife with an SUV for her birthday.

Focus Questions

- What kinds of associations were made? (Antonyms, synonyms, etc.)
- Did the fast pace help or hurt your response?
- How did you think of creative associations?
- What kind of associations were the most interesting?
- When making associations for the stories, how did you go about having two very different words make sense?

Avoid synonyms!

Type: Whole group/Improv
Skill: Beginning
Group Size: 5
Equipment: None

We play this game because:

Sometimes creativity demands that we bypass logic and come up with unusual associations.

Emphasis:

Blocking and Conventions
Characterization
Concentration
Creativity
Ensemble Acting
Following Directions
Give and Take Focus
Group Dynamics
Listening and Silence
Memorization
Nonverbal Communication
Observation
Physical Control
Plot Structure
Spontaneity
Storytelling

DEMO **5** MINUTES

PLAYER PREP **0** MINUTES

PERFORMANCE **10+** MINUTES

Type: Whole group/Improv
Skill: Beginning
Group Size: Whole group
Equipment: Noisemakers
(optional)

We play this game because:

Understanding how sounds can go together to create environments is essential.

Emphasis:

Blocking and Conventions

Characterization

Concentration

Creativity

Ensemble Acting

Following Directions

Give and Take Focus

Group Dynamics

Listening and Silence

Memorization

Nonverbal Communication

Observation

Physical Control

Plot Structure

Spontaneity

Storytelling

Directions

- Director distributes noisemakers if they will be used. Players are encouraged to use their voices, hands, etc., to make appropriate sounds.
- Group sits in a circle with eyes closed.
- Director suggests a sound environment and taps random players on their heads to add sounds to the environment.

Examples

- A Noisy Classroom: Sounds could include a bell ringing, tapping of pencils, coughing, nose blowing, teacher calling for quiet, whispering, etc.
- A Beach: Sounds could include kids calling to each other, waves splashing, seagulls, a hot dog salesman, catcalls, whistles, dogs barking, etc.
- An Emergency Room in a Large City Hospital: Sounds could include the drip of an IV, the beep of a heart monitor, paging for a doctor, moans, complaints, rustles.
- A Haunted House: Sounds could include an owl hooting, wind, rain, evil laughs, creaks, groans, and chains rattling.

Focus Questions

- Did the overall effect create an environment?
- Were there changes in the mood?
- Did all the sounds support the environment?
- Were there ever too many sounds?

Stress that all players need to listen and blend their sound with the others. Be sure not to tap too many players.

Suspense

DEMO
0
MINUTES

PLAYER PREP
5
MINUTES

PERFORMANCE
5
MINUTES

Directions

- Divide into groups of five.
- Each group draws six to ten sound effects.
- The groups get five minutes to plan a suspenseful radio drama using only their voices to create the dialog and sound effects.
- The radio drama should be amplified and performed out of sight of the audience if possible.
- The radio drama should be no longer than three minutes and must create suspense.

Examples

Using a car crash, wolves howling, doorbell chime, door creaking, door slamming, and a hooting owl, a scene is created in which a group of teenagers get into an accident and have to walk to an old deserted house to try to get help. Once there, they are trapped.

Focus Questions

- How did the sound effects contribute to the overall mood?
- How were you able to build suspense through the use of these sound effects?
- Did you find that the overall plot was enhanced by having sound effects as well as dialog?

You can find a helpful list in *Improv Ideas*:
Generic Scenes — Page 71
Sound Effects — Page 147

Type: Prepared
Skill: Intermediate
Group Size: 5
Equipment: Lists of situations, an upturned table to perform behind

We play this game because:
Background sounds can greatly enhance a scene.

Emphasis:

Blocking and Conventions
Characterization
Concentration
Creativity
Ensemble Acting
Following Directions
Give and Take Focus
Group Dynamics
Listening and Silence
Memorization
Nonverbal Communication
Observation
Physical Control
Plot Structure
Spontaneity
Storytelling

Integrative Projects

The following plans integrate the lessons learned from the weeks of improv and game playing. They last more than one day and end with a performance by each group for the class. Directors may choose to do one or more as time permits. We usually have time for all.

By this time the group should be acting as a cohesive whole and the director should know the strengths of the players. We strongly recommend allowing groups to form naturally, but also believe that a little discreet directorial tweaking of group composition can make for a more satisfying end product.

Storytelling/Urban Legends Project

Storytelling — Urban Legends I

Emphasis: Identifying how an urban legend gets started.

Equipment: Books of urban legends

Hint: Remind players of how a story can be twisted through constant retellings. Then discuss and "create" an urban legend. (See appendix, page 215).

Telephone (See page 31)	**Minutes: 10-15**

Listening closely is an essential drama skill.

Urban Legend Game	**Minutes: 40-50**

In reality, urban legends (and often horror movies) come from ordinary situations that are exaggerated.

Storytelling — Urban Legends II

Emphasis: Sharing urban legends heard from friends or other sources.

Equipment: Books of urban legends

Hint: These urban legends may be local or well known. Performers may bring in books as well. Use the broad categories of urban legends in the Appendix (page 215) to classify the stories shared.

Players Share Urban Legends	**Minutes: 50-60**

Most places have local urban legends, so it is always good to start with these as players sit around an imaginary campfire.

The Urban Legend Game

DEMO **0** MINUTES

PLAYER PREP **0** MINUTES

PERFORMANCE **40+** MINUTES

Type: Whole group
Skill: Intermediate
Group Size: Whole group
Equipment: None

We play this game because:

In reality, urban legends come from ordinary situations that are exaggerated.

Emphasis:

Blocking and Conventions

Characterization

Concentration

Creativity

Ensemble Acting

Following Directions

Give and Take Focus

Group Dynamics

Listening and Silence

Memorization

Nonverbal Communication

Observation

Physical Control

Plot Structure

Spontaneity

Storytelling

Discuss

Review plot elements: setting, rising action, conflict, climax, and conclusion.

Directions

- Group sits in a circle. The director starts with a "suggestion" sentence.
- Each group member adds an eerie element to the story by adding one sentence at a time.
- The "legend" should conclude with the second-to-last person in the circle.
- The last person adds a "moral" of the story.
- The director gives a new "suggestion" sentence, chooses a new player in the circle to begin, and the play repeats.

Example Suggestion Sentences

- An old lady who lived alone in a big city apartment was shivering in bed with the flu.
- Two teenagers decided to go to a dance in the next town even though there was a flood warning.
- The Johnson family was surprised but pleased that the old house cost so little.

Focus Questions

- Was it easy to come up with a spooky atmosphere?
- When was the conflict created?
- Did conflicts lead to a climax?
- Were there "red herrings"?
- Were there clearly-established characters?
- Were the conflicts driven by the plot or the characters?
- Was there a beginning, middle, and ending?
- Was it difficult to end the story?
- Did the moral of the story make sense?

Storytelling and Radio Drama Project

Storytelling and Radio Drama

Emphasis: Reviewing elements of urban legends and creating a generic story to act with sound and dialog.

Equipment: Books of urban legends

Hint: Referring to spoofs like the *Scary Movie* series, discuss which elements of plot/character are chosen to spoof/exaggerate and how these recognizable traits comprise many urban legends.

Elements of Urban Legends — Minutes: 10-15

Discuss what goes into an urban legend in terms of character, plot, and setting.

Generic Scenes — Minutes: 40-50

Choose a generic scene and improvise a five-minute radio drama using only voices and handmade sound effects.

Radio Drama — Listening

Emphasis: Listening to radio dramas and discussing the genre and what was achieved.

Equipment: Prerecorded radio dramas

Hint: Listening without the aid of video is often difficult for younger players. Discuss how it is possible to create pictures in the mind.

Listen to Prerecorded Radio Dramas — Minutes: 50-60

Listen to classics such as *The Whistler* and *The Shadow* to identify how the story is enhanced by the sound effects.

Storytelling and Radio Drama Project (Continued)

Radio Drama — Sound Effects

Emphasis: Evaluating the use and effectiveness of recorded theme music and sound effects.

Equipment: Recorded sound effects, player, noisemakers

Hint: Using available resources is a valuable skill. Make sure that there are some objects in the room such as meter sticks, tin cans, etc.

Listen to Sound Effects   Minutes: 15-20
Listen to and discuss the use of various sound effects.

Make Sound Effects   Minutes: 40-45
Find objects in the room with which to make homemade sound effects. Demonstrate.

Suspense Radio Drama

Emphasis: Discussing suspense and choosing a suspenseful story for a radio drama.

Equipment: Books of scary stories and urban legends

Hint: Go through two or three "stock" stories and decide as a class how these would be effectively cast.

Review Suspense Stories and Urban Legends   Minutes: 20-30
Recap the shared stories with a focus on which might be adapted to a radio drama format. Stress the difference between a narrated story and the dialog in a radio drama.

Choose a Story to Adapt for a Radio Drama   Minutes: 20-30
Choose stories that lend themselves to suspenseful presentation.

Storytelling and Radio Drama Project (Continued)

Radio Drama Scriptwriting

May take 3+ class periods

Emphasis: Creating a coherent radio drama plot with a clear conflict and well-defined characters.

Equipment: Paper, pens, pencils, books, chairs, tables, desks

Hint: The director should move around the room giving support and guidance to each group.

Each Day:

Writing Radio Scripts — Minutes: 45
In groups, students write radio scripts.

Processing Each Group's Progress — Minutes: 10-15
Check each group's specific progress in the large group. This is a time to share ideas and use group problem-solving skills to help individual groups.

Radio Drama Rehearsal

May take 3 class periods

Emphasis: Groups select appropriate theme music and sound effects and rehearse with them.

Equipment: Sound effects and theme music tapes/CDs, one player per group, noisemakers

Hint: Coordinating sound effects to the script requires great precision and many rehearsals to get it right! Encourage players to stay on task and take their time with this process.

Day 1 — Minutes: 45
Select sound effects and theme music for radio drama.
Progress reports to whole group. **Minutes: 10**

Days 2 and 3 — Minutes: 45
Rehearse radio drama with sound effects.
Progress reports to whole group. **Minutes: 10**

Storytelling and Radio Drama Project (Continued)

Radio Drama Performance

May take 3+ class periods

Emphasis: Performing and being a receptive audience for peers; critiquing a performance.

Equipment: Sound effects and theme music tapes/CDs, one player per group, noisemakers

Hint: Go over hints for effective critiques on page 4 before beginning any performances. Stress specific criticism.

Each Day:

Performances   Minutes: 40

Performances should be *no more* than ten minutes each. Limit performances to three per day.

Critiques   Minutes: 20

Critique after each performance. Spend approximately five minutes critiquing each performance.

Suspense Radio Drama

DEMO
AS NEEDED

PLAYER PREP
3-5
DAYS

PERFORMANCE
5-7
MINUTES

Directions

- Divide into small writing/performance groups of two to five.
- Each group chooses a story to adapt into a radio drama. (See Urban Legends in Appendix, page 215.)
- The group members choose characters in the story that they will portray. Some players may need to play several different characters depending on the number needed.
- The group chooses a recorder to write down dialog and sound effects suggested by the group.
- The groups write dialog for a five- to seven-minute suspenseful radio drama. (This process usually takes at least three class periods. Often one of the group members types the script at home and brings copies for all cast members. Other groups use a laptop in class, and members take turns typing the script.)
- When the groups each have a completed script, they may choose prerecorded sound effects and theme music, and they may plan homemade sounds.
- Groups get one to two class periods to rehearse their scripts with sounds effects.
- Each group performs for the entire class. Performances usually take place behind flats, curtains, or even a table on its side.
- Class and director critique each group's performance.

Focus Questions

- Did the radio drama tell a cohesive story with a beginning, middle, and ending?
- Did the plot create suspense?
- Did each individual character have a unique voice?
- Were you able to distinguish between the individual voices?
- Were sound effects and theme music used effectively?

Type: Prepared
Skill: Advanced
Group Size: 2-5
Equipment: : Pencils, paper, CD players, CDs with sound effects and theme music, audio tape players with microphones, blank audiotapes, noisemakers

We play this game because:

Creating suspense by using a scripted story (original or adapted), dialog, and sound effects synthesizes many drama skills.

Emphasis:

Blocking and Conventions
Characterization
Concentration
Creativity
Ensemble Acting
Following Directions
Give and Take Focus
Group Dynamics
Listening and Silence
Memorization
Nonverbal Communication
Observation
Physical Control
Plot Structure
Spontaneity
Storytelling

Puppet Spoofs Project

Puppet Spoofs Creation

May take 2 class periods

Emphasis: Creation of a parody using puppets as actors.

Equipment: Puppets, puppet stage or other masking

Hint: Puppets often create great enthusiasm. Be sure to stress puppet etiquette by modeling how to handle them properly.

Puppets can be made or purchased. If you choose to make puppets as part of the project, plan time for construction. A treasure hunt before the activity usually provides all the materials you will need. (See appendix page 218.)

Demonstration of Puppetry	**Minutes: 10**
Demonstrate puppet etiquette and proper handling.	
Discussion of Spoofs, Parody, Satire	**Minutes: 10**
Discuss elements of spoofs, parody, and satire, as well as well-known movies and TV shows that utilize this form of comedy.	
Create and Rehearse Puppet Spoofs	**Minutes: 35**
Each group plans a three- to five-minute puppet spoof.	

Puppet Spoofs Performance

Emphasis: Performing for peers; being a receptive audience for a performance by peers.

Equipment: Puppets, puppet stage or other masking

Hint: Stress critique etiquette once more. Critiques serve to celebrate the creative and excellent as well as to note areas for improvement. In fact, if there is not an opportunity to repeat the performance and you have distributed a basis for grades, you might want to forgo negative comments entirely.

Short Practice of Spoof	**Minutes: 5**
Groups quickly rehearse their spoofs.	
Performance and Critiques of Puppet Spoofs	**Minutes: 45**
Groups perform for the class, and each performance is critiqued.	

Puppet Spoofs

DEMO
5+
MINUTES

PLAYER PREP
30
MINUTES

PERFORMANCE
3-5
MINUTES

Directions

- Director "introduces" the group to a collection of hand puppets by holding up various puppets and performing different voices and attitudes for each.
- Director asks for volunteers to voice certain puppets.
- Group critiques how the voices matched the appearance of the puppets.
- Director leads group in discussion of spoofs. Spoofs must have exaggerated plots and characters.
- Group divides into small groups of five.
- Each member of the group gets one to four puppets depending on availability. (Two puppets each is ideal.)
- Each group decides on a spoof. Spoofs can be of existing stories, films, TV shows, or situations. (See appendix, page 217.)
- Each group gets thirty minutes to prepare a three- to five-minute spoof of an episode from the story.
- The next day, the groups get a few minutes to review, then they perform for each other. The class critiques each performance.

Examples

- *Harry Potter*: Harry is a juvenile delinquent who is incarcerated in a school for students with behavior problems. He and his friends, Weasel and Ranger, are always getting into trouble.
- *Dawn of the Dead*: A group of innocent zombies is trying to live peacefully in a shopping mall, feeding off Burger King and McDonald's garbage. They are attacked by a group of holiday shoppers gone berserk.

Focus Questions

- Which aspects of the story were spoofed?
- Did the episode as developed make sense?
- Was the spoof humorous?
- Did the voices fit the puppets?
- Did the puppets fit the characters they were supposed to represent?
- Were the puppets themselves part of the spoof? (Which puppets were chosen to represent which characters?)

Type: Prepared
Skill: Intermediate/Advanced
Group Size: 5
Equipment: Puppets, puppet stage or other masking

We play this game because:

Since spoofs are exaggerations of character and plot they are perfect prompts to use for puppetry.

Emphasis:

Blocking and Conventions
Characterization
Concentration
Creativity
Ensemble Acting
Following Directions
Give and Take Focus
Group Dynamics
Listening and Silence
Memorization
Nonverbal Communication
Observation
Physical Control
Plot Structure
Spontaneity
Storytelling

Puppet Choreography Project

Puppet Choreography Intro

Emphasis: Using stage awareness techniques and basic choreography moves for puppet musical numbers.

Equipment: Puppets, puppet stage, recorded music, players for each group

Hint: Puppets and rhythm seem to go together. Your collection of fun songs and interesting puppets will have players thrilled to select puppets and get going with their own projects.

Puppet Choreography Demonstration   Minutes: 10-15
Demonstrate a variety of puppet movement options.

Selection of Music and Rehearsal   Minutes: 30
Groups select music and begin to plan their performances.

Puppet Choreography Rehearsal

May take 2 class periods

Emphasis: Working as a group to make informed and creative decisions.

Equipment: Puppets, puppet stage, recorded music, players for each group

Hint: This is also a time to work on costume elements for the puppets if desired.

Rehearsal for Puppet Choreography   Minutes: 40
Plan each move for its theatrical impact. Group members should take turns being the director as they look for blocking that works best for their song.

Progress Reports to the Entire Group   Minutes: 15
Check each group's specific progress in the large group. Share ideas and use group problem-solving skills to help individual groups.

Puppet Choreography Project (Continued)

Puppet Choreography Performance

May take 2 class periods

Emphasis: Performing for peers. Being a receptive audience for a performance by peers.

Equipment: Puppets, puppet stage, recorded music, players for each group

Hint: It is important to have a variety of puppet movements (up and down, side to side, diagonal lines, straight "chorus" lines, level differences, etc.) Stress that not all puppets have to be on-stage at the same time.

Performance of Puppet Choreography   Minutes: 45
Groups perform their puppet choreography skits.

Critiques of Puppet Choreography   Minutes: 15
Critique after each performance. Critiques should last approximately three minutes each.

Music Video

Emphasis: Applying organizing techniques from *Radio Drama* and staging techniques from *Puppet Choreography* to live performance.

Equipment: Recorded music, players for each group; video recording capability; paper, markers, scissors for backgrounds; basic costumes if desired

Hint: Keep the emphasis on presenting what the players have been working on. This was not a stagecraft or costume class — downplay those elements.

Apply the techniques learned in the *Puppet Choreography* unit to a *Music Video* (Human Choreography) unit. Use recorded music and allow players who are interested to "sing along," but stress that the emphasis is on staging, NOT lip-syncing.

Scenery may be made with butcher paper and cardboard from boxes.

Costumes — if used — should be basic.

Plan at least a week for introduction, rehearsal, scenic creation, and preliminary video recording.

Video record the performances before the live audience of fellow players and critique the videotapes.

Puppet Choreography

DEMO
10+
MINUTES

PLAYER PREP
30
MINUTES

PERFORMANCE
2-3
MINUTES

Type: Prepared
Skill: Advanced
Group Size: 2-5
Equipment: Puppets, puppet stage, recorded music, players for each group

We play this game because:

There is a great deal of variety that can be utilized when working with simple hand puppets. This variety transfers to human acting.

Emphasis:

Blocking and Conventions

Characterization

Concentration

Creativity

Ensemble Acting

Following Directions

Give and Take Focus

Group Dynamics

Listening and Silence

Memorization

Nonverbal Communication

Observation

Physical Control

Plot Structure

Spontaneity

Storytelling

Directions

- Director demonstrates a variety of puppet movement options with four volunteers and eight to ten puppets.
- Group listens to a song and discusses options for staging.
- Group divides into small groups of two to five, choose songs, and plan staging.
- Groups perform for and critique one another the next day.

Focus Questions

- Did the groups use variety in choreography and staging?
- Was it easy to tell what characters the puppets represented?
- Did the puppets' mouths move to the words of the song?
- Were the movements appropriate to tell the story?
- Did the movements fit the characters' roles in the song?
- Was the performance visually interesting?
- Were certain words or phrases emphasized with movement?

The Answers at the Back of the Book

Box Games We Love

We love board games and often get ideas from them! These are just a few of our all time favorites! Use in small groups or adapt to the entire class. Enjoy.

Game	Publisher
AdVersity	Fundex Games
Apples to Apples	Out of the Box Publishing
Argue!	University Games
Articulate!	University Games
Balderdash	Mattel
Best of Tribond	Mattel
Blurt!	Mattel
The Charade Game	Pressman Toy
Cranuim	Cranium
Faces	Buffalo Games, Inc.
Fact or Crap	University Games
Fib or Not?	Gather Around Games
Guesstures	Milton Bradley
iMAgiNiff…	Buffalo Games, Inc.
Last Word	Buffalo Games, Inc.
Loaded Questions	All Things Equal, Inc.
Mad Gab	Mattel
Outburst	Mattel
Scattergories	Milton Bradley
Scruples	Catalyst Games
Snorta!	Out of the Box Publishing
Spinergy®	GnuGames, Inc.
Taboo	Milton Bradley
Urban Myth	Rumba Games

Vocabulary for Improv and Rehearsal

The emphasis of this book is learning theatre through drama games and improvisation, and much of the language is specific to that process. The end result, though, is an appreciation of and the ability to create many forms of theatre: improvisational and unscripted, playwriting, and working with scripted works. Below is a vocabulary list. Concepts specific to improvisation are introduced in all caps.

ACCEPTING AN OFFER: Embracing an action or dialog presented by other players.

Advancing: The process of moving a scene forward with action or dialog.

BLOCKING AN OFFER: Refusing to play or changing the ideas offered; any action in an improv that does not carry the improv forward.

Blocking (play production): The management of physical action in the playing space. What part of the stage is used and why; the use of props and furniture and the ways players move in the playing space are all part of blocking.

Conflict: The problem presented in the work. It is between or among characters or forces and shapes or motivates the action of the plot. Typical conflicts are between individuals; between groups; between an individual and society, nature, or an inanimate object; or internal in one character.

Conventions: The practices that make improvisations and theatrical productions successful for both actors and audience. Speaking loudly enough to be heard by fellow players and audience, facing the audience most of the time, and giving and taking focus are conventions.

Climax: The moment of greatest dramatic intensity; the turning point in the action.

Crisis: A moment of high dramatic intensity; a turning point in the action, usually followed by a decrease in suspense. (The final crisis is the climax.)

Denouement (day-no-mah): The unraveling of the plot, following the climax, in which the players show how and why everything turned out as it did. A denouement is unnecessary for many short improvs.

Director: Group leaders, teachers, or play directors. Players may also serve as directors for games.

Ensemble: A group constituting an organic whole or working together for a single effect.

ENDOWMENT: A player or players giving attributes to another player's character. The endowed attribute must be discovered and/or adapted to.

Exposition: The background information that reveals "how it all began" — namely, what happened prior to the time covered in the improv, what the characters are like, and what situation has arisen that will lead to a problem that must be solved.

Focus: The person or thing that receives the attention of both the players and the audience. Shifting focus is a hallmark of an interesting scene.

GIVE AND TAKE: Dialog and focus going back and forth between players.

Inciting incident (or episode): The incident that changes the story forever. The point at which there is no turning back in the story; things will never be the same.

Monolog: A solo actor speaking directly to the audience.

Narrative: The story told by the scene.

Narration: A speech introducing or underlying a scene, usually offering information not available in the action. Usually narration is discouraged because it is better to show than tell. In improv, this device may be used to give actors information upon which to act.

OFFER: Action or dialog presented by a player that advances the scene.

Players: The participants in the improvs. Players may be actors or members of a recreational group.

Playing Space: The area in which you perform — be it stage, raised platform, or part of the room.

Plot: The series of events or episodes that make up the action of the improv or play. (See exposition, inciting incident, rising action, climax, and denouement.)

Rising action: The series of events, preceding the climax, which intensify the conflict and, thereby, create a feeling of suspense about the outcome.

Setting: The background time, place, weather, and circumstances in which the events in an improv take place.

Side Coaching: Providing a player with added information about the character or the scene. The director or coach provides this during the scene. The players act upon the side coaching but do not actively acknowledge it.

Soliloquy: A lone character speaking his/her thoughts aloud.

Status: A character's sense of self-esteem or organizational or social standing to which they naturally adhere.

Storytelling: Developing the story line (plot) in a logical manner.

Subtext: The aspects of the character that are not specifically stated in the improv or script but are the underlying reasons for the character's actions at the moment of the playing.

WAFFLING: Postponing the progress of the improv because of lack of ideas or choice of an idea to use.

WIMPING: Acknowledging offers but refusing to add to them.

Charades

Goal: To silently act out a word or phrase to be guessed by other players.

Rules: Words may be acted out in order, or the player may choose the key word to act out first. The player may also choose to act out the entire title or phrase. Words may be broken into syllables.

Standard Gestures for Charades

Category

Book title: Unfold your hands as if they were a book.

Movie title: Pretend to crank an old-fashioned movie camera.

Person: Stand erect and pose like Napoleon.

Play title: Pretend to pull the rope that opens a theatre curtain.

Song title: Pretend to sing.

TV show: Draw a rectangle to outline the TV screen.

Quote or phrase: Make quotation marks in the air with your fingers.

Words: Pretend to type on a keyboard.

About the words

Number of words: Hold up the number of fingers.

Which word you're working on: Hold up the number of fingers again.

Length of word: Make a "little" or "big" sign as if you were measuring a fish.

Number of syllables in the word: Lay the number of fingers on your arm.

Syllable you're working on: Lay the number of fingers on your arm again.

Letter of the alphabet: (Try to avoid this one — it's a game, not a spelling bee.) Move your hand in a chopping motion toward your arm (near the top of your forearm if the letter is near the beginning of the alphabet, and near the bottom of your arm if the letter is near the end of the alphabet).

Other Helpful Gestures

Correct: Nod and point at person who got the right answer.

You're on the right track, keep trying: Beckon person who gets a close answer, nodding as they get closer.

All of it: Sweep your arms through the air.

Longer version of: Stretch with hand (think taffy).

Past tense: Wave hand toward back (think of putting it behind you).

Plural: Link index fingers (these go together).

Shorter version of: Compress with your hand (think a soft rubber ball).

Sounds like: Cup one hand behind an ear.

FYI

What you need to play.

	Time Per Group

Page	Title	Players/group	Equipment	Demo	Player Prep	Performance
69	Accident, The	4	N	0	10	3
101	Add a Where	2	Y	0	0	15
89	Addition and Subtraction	5	N	5	0	15
98	Alphabet Game	2	N	0	0	15
142	Alter Egos	4	Y	0	0	2
168	Anchorman	4	Y	0	15	5
35	As If …	W	N	0	0	5
172	Bad Guy/Good Guy	2	Y	0	5	2
36	Blind Walk	2	Y	0	0	15
75	Change It!	W	N	5	0	10
58	Change Three Things	W	N	0	0	15
14	Charades	W	Y	0	0	2
137	Conflict Game	2	N	5	3	3
178	CSI: Your Hometown	4	Y	0	10	5
149	Death in a Restaurant	6	Y	5	0	10
150	Dubbing	4	Y	0	0	20
37	Duck, Duck, Goose	W	N	0	0	15
123	Duo Stage Directions	2	Y	10	5	45
133	Elevator	3	N	5	10	3
62	Emotional Freezes	3	Y	0	10	3
96	Exchange Student/Translators	2	N	5	0	2
61	Family Portraits	5	Y	5	10	5
151	Film Critics	5	Y	0	0	20
83	First Line, Last Line	2	Y	5	5	1
160	Flashback	5	Y	0	10	5
162	Fractured Fairy Tales	4	N	0	5	5
66	Freeze Titles	5	Y	2	0	5
25	Frog and Fly	W	Y	0	0	20
16	Fruit Basket Upset	W	Y	0	0	15
152	Genre House	2	Y	0	0	3
135	Getting There Is Half the Fun	4	Y	0	10	3
97	Gibberish	2	N	0	0	10
91	Gimme a Hand	4	N	0	0	5
76	Gimme That Seat	5	Y	0	0	10
90	Happy Hands	2	N	10	0	3
92	Hats	3	Y	5	10	1
28	Hi, How Are You?	W	N	5	0	5
174	Hitchhiker	5	Y	0	0	2
42	Hunter and Hunted	W	Y	0	0	10
107	I'm a Little Teapot	1	Y	5	10	1
15	I'm Going on a Trip	W	N	0	0	20
88	I've Got It, You Want It	2	Y	0	0	10
140	If I Were a Skunk	2	N	1	0	2
105	Impromptu	1	N	3	.5	1
102	In A … With A …	2	N	3	0	1
103	In A … With A … While A …	2	N	0	0	1
95	In a Manner of Speaking	2	N	0	0	3
155	In the Style Of	3	N	0	0	3
166	Invention Of, The	3	N	0	3	3
39	It Ain't Heavy, It's …	W	N	5	0	10
48	It Wasn't My Fault	W	N	0	0	15
163	It's All in the Point of View	4	N	0	15	5
17	Key Chains	W	Y	0	0	15
78	Line at a Time	10	N	0	0	10
13	Line Up by Height	W	N	0	0	10
53	Machine Game, The	5	N	5	5	3
51	Make an Entrance	1	Y	10	0	15
85	Make Me Do It	2	Y	0	0	10
110	Master Servant	2	N	2	0	2
54	Metaphor Machine, The	5	N	5	10	3
41	Mirror Game	2	N	5	0	10
165	Mix and Match	4	Y	0	10	2
125	Mixed Motivations	2	N	5	10	2
64	Movie Theatre	5	Y	0	10	5
177	Murder in the Dark	W	N	0	0	50
153	Musical Improv	2	Y	5	0	5
21	Name Ball	W	Y	0	0	10
20	Name Game	W	N	0	0	15
27	Newsies	W	Y	0	0	10
146	Next-Door Neighbors, The	3	Y	0	3	3
57	Objects on a Tray	W	Y	0	0	15
115	Obsessed With	2	Y	0	3	5

FYI

What you need to play.

Page		Players/group	Equipment	Demo	Player Prep	Performance
32	One-Sentence-at-a-Time Story	W	Y	0	0	15
129	Opening and Closing Scenes	1	N	0	0	20
86	Park Bench	6	Y	0	0	10
47	Party Mix	W	Y	0	0	5
114	Party Quirk Endowments	5	Y	0	0	5
55	Pass the Object	W	Y	0	0	5
56	Pass the Stick	W	Y	0	0	5
156	Past/Present/Future	4	N	5	5	3
73	Phone Booth	5	N	0	0	10
30	Poop Deck	W	Y	0	0	15
63	Props Freeze	5	Y	5	3	3
196	Puppet Choreography	2	Y	10	30	2
193	Puppet Spoofs	5	Y	5	30	3
120	Roommate	2	Y	2	3	5
72	School Bus	9	Y	0	0	10
34	Sensing	W	N	0	0	15
117	Sick	2	N	2	1	1
23	Simon Says	W	N	0	0	5
45	Slow-Motion Commentary	2	N	0	0	20
44	Slow-Motion Explosion Tag	2	N	5	0	15
43	Slow-Motion Fighting	2	N	5	0	15
122	Solo Stage Directions	1	Y	5	0	40
29	Sound Ball	W	Y	2	0	5
106	SPAR (Spontaneous Argumentation)	2	Y	10	15	6
159	Spinergy®	4	Y	5	2	3
136	Standing, Sitting, Kneeling	5	Y	5	0	10
109	Status Bench	10	Y	0	0	5
111	Status Slide	2	Y	5	0	5
173	Stop and Go	6	Y	0	0	15
77	Story, Story, Die	5	N	0	0	20
145	Stupid, Smelly, Sexy	4	N	5	0	5
181	Suspense	5	Y	0	5	5
191	Suspense Radio Drama	2	Y	0	60+	5
71	Take Focus	5	Y	3	0	3
128	Tap In (Milwaukee Freeze Tag)	W	N	5	0	25
31	Telephone	W	N	0	0	15

Page		Players/group	Equipment	Demo	Player Prep	Performance
79	TMATTY	1	Y	0	0	1
180	This Sounds Like the Place	W	Y	5	0	10
143	Time Out	4	N	5	10	3
157	Time Portal	3	Y	0	1	2
171	To the Rescue	2	N	3	5	2
169	Today's Your Lucky Day	4	Y	3	0	5
50	Transformations	1	N	3	0	5
134	Trapped	3	N	3	5	3
18	Truth or Lie?	W	Y	5	0	20
87	Twisted	3	Y	0	0	.5
186	Urban Legend Game, The	W	N	0	0	40
118	Values	2	Y	10	10	2
141	Wacky Family, The	4	N	0	3	2
38	Walking	W	N	0	0	10
68	Wax Museum	5	Y	0	10	3
126	We Don't See Eye-to-Eye	2	N	0	2	2
130	What Comes Next?	2	N	0	0	5
116	What's My Line?	4	Y	2	0	5
144	What's Your Sign?	2	Y	0	0	3
100	Where Game, The	W	N	5	0	10
24	Who Started the Motion?	W	N	0	0	10
84	Whose Line	2	Y	5	0	10
179	Word Association	5	N	0	0	20
80	Word Tennis	2	Y	3	0	10
65	Yearbook Game	5	Y	0	1	20
49	Yes, And ...	W	Y	0	0	3
94	Yes/No – One-Word Scenes	2	N	0	0	10
22	You!	W	N	5	0	10
119	You've Got a Secret	2	Y	0	0	5

Dramatic Uses for Games

The following charts provide a quick reference for those planning to use games to fit a particular drama lesson or rehearsal.

Page	Game	Blocking and Conventions	Characterization	Concentration	Creativity	Ensemble Acting	Following Directions	Give and Take Focus	Group Dynamics	Listening and Silence	Memorization	Nonverbal Communication	Observation	Physical Control	Plot Structure	Spontaneity	Storytelling
							To Teach and Practice										
69	Accident, The											•		•	•		
101	Add a Where				•	•									•		
89	Addition and Subtraction							•							•		
98	Alphabet Game			•	•												•
142	Alter Egos		•			•											
168	Anchorman					•									•		
35	As If …		•			•						•				•	
172	Bad Guy/Good Guy		•			•									•		
36	Blind Walk					•						•					
75	Change It!				•	•										•	
58	Change Three Things			•					•				•				
14	Charades											•		•			
137	Conflict Game					•									•		
178	CSI: Your Hometown	•				•									•		
149	Death in a Restaurant		•			•	•	•								•	
150	Dubbing					•								•	•		
37	Duck, Duck, Goose			•					•					•			
123	Duo Stage Directions	•				•									•		
133	Elevator					•									•		
62	Emotional Freezes					•						•					
96	Exchange Student/Translators					•				•						•	

Dramatic Uses for Games (Continued)

Page	Game	Blocking and Conventions	Characterization	Concentration	Creativity	Ensemble Acting	Following Directions	Give and Take Focus	Group Dynamics	Listening and Silence	Memorization	Nonverbal Communication	Observation	Physical Control	Plot Structure	Spontaneity	Storytelling
									To Teach and Practice								
61	Family Portraits		•		•							•					
151	Film Critics				•										•	•	
83	First Line, Last Line				•										•		
160	Flashback			•											•		
162	Fractured Fairy Tales		•			•									•		
66	Freeze Titles		•			•						•				•	
25	Frog and Fly			•			•		•								
16	Fruit Basket Upset						•									•	
152	Genre House					•									•	•	
135	Getting There Is Half the Fun					•								•	•		
97	Gibberish		•	•	•												
91	Gimme a Hand				•	•								•			
76	Gimme That Seat				•	•										•	
90	Happy Hands		•		•											•	
92	Hats		•												•		
28	Hi, How Are You?				•					•						•	
174	Hitchhiker		•			•										•	
42	Hunter and Hunted			•									•	•			
107	I'm a Little Teapot		•		•												
15	I'm Going on a Trip							•			•						
88	I've Got It, You Want It				•	•										•	

Dramatic Uses for Games (Continued)

Page	Game	Blocking and Conventions	Characterization	Concentration	Creativity	Ensemble Acting	Following Directions	Give and Take Focus	Group Dynamics	Listening and Silence	Memorization	Nonverbal Communication	Observation	Physical Control	Plot Structure	Spontaneity	Storytelling
							To Teach and Practice										
140	If I Were a Skunk		•			•						•					
105	Impromptu				•										•	•	
102	In A … With A …				•	•										•	
103	In A … With A … While A …				•										•	•	
95	In a Manner of Speaking		•												•	•	
155	In the Style Of				•	•										•	
166	Invention Of, The			•	•										•		
39	It Ain't Heavy, It's …				•							•		•			
48	It Wasn't My Fault			•	•											•	
163	It's All in the Point of View		•												•		
17	Key Chains				•				•				•		•		•
78	Line at a Time				•											•	
13	Line Up by Height						•		•	•			•				
53	Machine Game, The				•	•						•		•		•	
51	Make an Entrance	•			•		•										
85	Make Me Do It						•		•							•	
110	Master Servant		•			•											
54	Metaphor Machine, The				•	•										•	
41	Mirror Game				•							•	•	•			
165	Mix and Match		•			•									•	•	
125	Mixed Motivations		•			•									•		

Dramatic Uses for Games (Continued)

Page	Game	Blocking and Conventions	Characterization	Concentration	Creativity	Ensemble Acting	Following Directions	Give and Take Focus	Group Dynamics	Listening and Silence	Memorization	Nonverbal Communication	Observation	Physical Control	Plot Structure	Spontaneity	Storytelling
							To Teach and Practice										
64	Movie Theatre		•			•						•			•		
177	Murder in the Dark			•		•			•								
153	Musical Improv				•											•	
21	Name Ball				•	•										•	
20	Name Game				•											•	
27	Newsies			•	•											•	
146	Next-Door Neighbors, The		•			•									•		
57	Objects on a Tray			•					•		•		•				
115	Obsessed With		•			•										•	
32	One-Sentence-at-a-Time Story				•	•										•	•
129	Opening and Closing Scenes			•								•			•		
86	Park Bench		•			•									•		
47	Party Mix		•			•			•								
114	Party Quirk Endowments		•			•										•	
55	Pass the Object		•						•			•		•			
56	Pass the Stick				•				•			•		•			
156	Past/Present/Future		•		•										•		
73	Phone Booth		•		•			•									
30	Poop Deck	•					•		•								
63	Props Freeze					•							•	•			
196	Puppet Choreography														•		

Dramatic Uses for Games (Continued)

Page	Game	Blocking and Conventions	Characterization	Concentration	Creativity	Ensemble Acting	Following Directions	Give and Take Focus	Group Dynamics	Listening and Silence	Memorization	Nonverbal Communication	Observation	Physical Control	Plot Structure	Spontaneity	Storytelling
							To Teach and Practice										
193	Puppet Spoofs		•			•									•		
120	Roommate		•		•	•											
72	School Bus	•				•						•					
34	Sensing			•								•	•				
117	Sick		•		•	•											
23	Simon Says					•	•					•					
45	Slow-Motion Commentary					•						•		•		•	
44	Slow-Motion Explosion Tag											•		•			
43	Slow-Motion Fighting					•								•			
122	Solo Stage Directions	•				•									•		
29	Sound Ball				•	•						•					
106	SPAR (Spontaneous Argumentation)					•										•	
159	Spinergy®					•			•							•	
136	Standing, Sitting, Kneeling				•	•										•	
109	Status Bench		•						•								
111	Status Slide		•			•										•	
173	Stop and Go					•									•	•	
77	Story, Story, Die			•		•									•	•	
145	Stupid, Smelly, Sexy		•			•										•	
181	Suspense					•						•				•	
191	Suspense Radio Drama		•			•									•		

Dramatic Uses for Games (Continued)

Page	Game	Blocking and Conventions	Characterization	Concentration	Creativity	Ensemble Acting	Following Directions	Give and Take Focus	Group Dynamics	Listening and Silence	Memorization	Nonverbal Communication	Observation	Physical Control	Plot Structure	Spontaneity	Storytelling
								To Teach and Practice									
71	Take Focus		•		•			•								•	
128	Tap In (Milwaukee Freeze Tag)		•	•											•		
31	Telephone						•		•	•							
79	TMATTY				•										•	•	•
180	This Sounds Like the Place				•	•										•	
143	Time Out		•						•						•		
157	Time Portal				•	•										•	
171	To the Rescue		•			•									•		
169	Today's Your Lucky Day		•												•	•	
50	Transformations		•									•		•			
134	Trapped					•									•		
18	Truth or Lie?				•				•						•		
87	Twisted		•		•	•										•	
186	Urban Legend Game, The				•										•		•
118	Values		•												•		
141	Wacky Family, The		•			•									•		
38	Walking				•							•		•			
68	Wax Museum					•							•	•	•		
126	We Don't See Eye-to-Eye		•			•									•		
130	What Comes Next?				•	•									•		
116	What's My Line?		•			•										•	

Dramatic Uses for Games (Continued)

Page	Game	Blocking and Conventions	Characterization	Concentration	Creativity	Ensemble Acting	Following Directions	Give and Take Focus	Group Dynamics	Listening and Silence	Memorization	Nonverbal Communication	Observation	Physical Control	Plot Structure	Spontaneity	Storytelling
							To Teach and Practice										
144	What's Your Sign?		•		•	•											
100	Where Game, The			•	•	•											
24	Who Started the Motion?			•		•								•			
84	Whose Line				•											•	•
179	Word Association								•							•	•
80	Word Tennis			•	•					•						•	
65	Yearbook Game				•				•			•					
49	Yes, And ...				•		•									•	
94	Yes/No – One-Word Scenes				•	•										•	
22	You!			•		•			•								
119	You've Got a Secret		•		•	•										•	

Stage Areas Map

Up Right	Up Center	Up Left
Center Right	Center	Center Left
Down Right	Down Center	Down Left

Audience

Persuasion and Propaganda Techniques (Use for SPAR on page 106.)

Use supporting evidence such as facts, examples, and expert opinions.

Distort the facts.

Use flattery.

Use the bandwagon approach of "everybody is doing it."

Use an excess of science.

Quote statistics and use them to mean what *you* want them to mean.

Use loaded phrases like "of course," "obviously," and "as you know."

Make an emotional appeal.

Use big words to imply that you are knowledgeable.

Say that a famous person or celebrity agrees with your point of view.

Use the "just plain folks" technique to identify your opinion with wholesome values.

Bring out negative feelings by name-calling.

Use glittering generalities that are so general that they cannot be disproved.

Tell people what they want to hear.

Link statements that do not necessarily follow.

Point out your opponent's weaknesses or the weaknesses of his argument.

Stack the deck. Tell all that's good about your argument and all that's bad about your opponent's.

Use and distort logic.

Idea Lists

Values

Accomplishment
Accountability
Accuracy
Adventure
Athleticism
Beauty
Being satisfied
Calm
Caution
Challenge
Change
Chastity
Cleanliness
Cleverness
Collaboration
Commitment
Communication
Community
Compassion
Competence
Competition
Cooperation
Creativity
Decisiveness
Democracy
Discipline
Discovery
Efficiency
Empathy
Equality
Esprit de corps
Excellence
Fair play

Fairness
Faith
Family
Fellowship
Fidelity
Friendship
Fun
Generosity
Goodwill
Goodness
Gratitude
Hard work
Harmony
Honesty
Honor
Humor
Independence
Integrity
Joy
Justice
Knowledge
Leadership
Love
Loyalty
Openness
Optimism
Patriotism
Perfection
Physical appearance
Pleasure
Power
Practicality
Privacy
Problem Solving

Progress
Punctuality
Resourcefulness
Respect
Responsiveness
Safety
Satisfaction
Scholarship
Security
Self-reliance
Selflessness
Serenity
Service
Simplicity
Sincerity
Skill
Solitude
Speed
Stability
Status
Strength
Success
Teamwork
Timeliness
Tolerance
Tradition
Tranquility
Trust
Truth
Unity
Variety
Wealth
Well-being
Wisdom

Astrological Signs

Western

Capricorn (December 22-January 20): Responsible, detail-oriented, likes tangible results, precise, persevering, practical, clear-minded, dutiful.

Aquarius (January 21-February 19): Independent, clever, objective, original, aloof, noncommittal, reserved, likes variety.

Pisces (February 20-March 20): Intuitive, flexible, self-sacrificing, insightful, wise, empathetic, devoted.

Aries (March 21-April 20): Resilient, energetic, spontaneous, impulsive, direct, easy-going, independent, arbitrary, optimistic, risk taker, wants own way.

Taurus (April 21-May 21): Practical, decisive, dependable, persevering, concrete thinker, faithful, stubborn, can be hot-tempered when really pushed.

Gemini (May 22-June 21): Versatile, happy, curious, talkative, clever, critical thinker, precise, quick-witted, social, restless.

Cancer (June 22-July 23): Romantic, caring, feeling, empathetic, home-loving, sensitive, impressionable, naïve, trusting, affectionate.

Leo (July 24-August 23): Decisive, risk taking, calm, self-reliant, intelligent, strong convictions, self-confident, passionate.

Virgo (August 24-September 23): Orderly, reliable, critical thinker, pragmatic, good with details, cautious, reserved, faithful.

Libra (September 24-October 23): Creative, impulsive, needs harmony and beauty, enterprising, tactful, sociable, needs freedom.

Scorpio (October 24-November 22): Uncompromising, provocative, strong-willed, cynical, enormous emotional strength, access to dark powers.

Sagittarius (November 23-December 21): Achiever, highly convicted, highly educated, far-reaching plans, enthusiastic, enjoys partnerships, loves travel.

Chinese

Rat (1972, 1984): Social, intellectual, skilled, charismatic, acquisitive, talkative, pleasant, good provider.

Ox (1973, 1985): Stable, innovative, eloquent, stubborn, hard worker, serious, diligent.

Tiger (1974, 1986): Impetuous, lucky, magnetic personality, passionate, honest.

Cat (1975, 1987): Virtuous, tactful, ambitious, refined, elegant, traditional.

Dragon (1976, 1987): Strong, successful, healthy, enthusiastic, sentimental, authoritative.

Snake (1977, 1989): Intuitive, attractive, discreet, thoughtful, successful.

Horse (1978, 1990): Popular, stylish, accomplished, independent, pragmatic.

Goat (1979, 1991): Inventive, sensitive, needs security, impractical, slow starter, well-mannered.

Monkey (1980, 1992): Cunning, enthusiastic, leader, charming, joker, problem solver.

Rooster (1982, 1993): Enthusiastic, conservative, humorous, stylish, helpful, security conscious.

Dog (1983, 1994): Constant, respectable, dutiful, moral, suspicious, intractable.

Pig (1984, 1995): Sincere, cultured, honest, strong, loving, luxury seeking, craves knowledge, hot-tempered.

Urban Legends

Alligators in the Sewer

Babysitter/The Call from the Upstairs Phone

Bloody Fingers

Bloody Mary

Boyfriend's Death/Don't Look Back

The Choking Doberman

The Hitchhiker

The Girl in White

The Hook

The Weeping Woman/*La Llorona*

Little White Dog/Drip! Drip!

The Mexican Pet

Murderer in the Back Seat

Outside the Door/Roommate's Death

Prom Dress/The Yellow Ribbon

Room for One More/The Elevator

Spiders in the Hairdo

Tailypo/The Dead Man's Hand

The Viper

The Wendigo

Generic Scenes for Urban Legends

It is a dark and stormy night. A group of friends are at a sleepover at the country home of one of the kid's grandparents. The grandparents are asleep in another part of the old house, so the kids decide to tell each other ghost stories. Suddenly, a creaking noise is heard, as if someone is slowly climbing up the stairs, trying not to be heard. The kids fall silent and listen. A few minutes later they hear it again, coming even closer.

What happens next?

Two friends are baby-sitting a neighbor's children. It is late at night, and the parents were expected to have returned a half hour before. Turning on the TV, the babysitters realize that there has been extensive flooding in the next town due to severe thunderstorms. They wonder if the parents were caught in the flood and why they haven't called. Suddenly, the phone rings. They answer it and there is someone groaning on the other end.

What happens next?

A brother and sister are visiting their aunt and uncle at their farm in the country. They are happy about this because their relatives have a wonderful dog named Max with whom the kids love to play. One night the aunt and uncle decide to go into town to visit some friends. They leave the kids with Max in the old house. It is getting late, and Max needs to go out. The kids let him into the yard. Suddenly, there is extensive barking. Then, all goes silent.

What happens next?

Four scouts on a camp out are alone in the woods. It starts to drizzle, so one of the scouts volunteers to go fetch wood for a fire. The rest of the kids bustle around preparing the tents and supplies. A half hour later their friend has still not returned. Then they start to hear mysterious rustlings in the bushes.

What happens next?

A boy and a girl are driving home on an old country road when their car hits something in the road. The boy gets out to see what he hit, but he can't see a thing as it is raining too hard and he doesn't have a flashlight. He thinks that he hears some sort of noise under the car, so he is afraid to drive off lest he hurt whatever, or whomever, he hit. He gets back in the car to tell his girlfriend and finds her absolutely panicked, insisting that they get out of there *now*.

What happens next?

Suggested Puppet Spoofs

Certain movies and TV shows are already spoofs so you cannot exaggerate in the direction they are already going. For example, to spoof *South Park* the kids would have to be extremely polite and conservative!

Fairy Tales	Films
Aladdin	*Crouching Tiger, Hidden Dragon*
Ali Baba and the Forty Thieves	*Dawn of the Dead*
Alice in Wonderland	*Die Hard*
Beauty and the Beast	*Dr. Dolittle*
Charlie and the Chocolate Factory	*Dracula*
Cinderella	*E.T. the Extra-Terrestrial*
Demeter and Persephone	*Frankenstein*
The Gingerbread Man	*Gone with the Wind*
Goldilocks and the Three Bears	*Halloween*
Hansel and Gretel	*Harry Potter*
The Hobbit	*Indiana Jones*
Jack and the Beanstalk	*It's a Wonderful Life*
James and the Giant Peach	*James Bond*
King Arthur	*Lethal Weapon*
King Midas	*The Lord of the Rings*
The Little Match Girl	*The Maltese Falcon*
The Little Mermaid	*Men in Black*
Little Red Riding Hood	*Miracle on 34th Street*
The Odyssey	*Mission: Impossible*
Oliver Twist	*The Mummy*
Perseus	*Scream*
Peter Rabbit	*Spiderman*
Rapunzel	*Star Trek*
Robin Hood	*Star Wars*
Rumpelstiltskin	*Titanic*
Sinbad	*War of the Worlds*
Sleeping Beauty	
Snow White	
The Three Billy Goats Gruff	
The Three Little Pigs	
The Velveteen Rabbit	
The Wizard of Oz	

TV Shows

Ally McBeal	*Lost*
Cheers	*Malcolm in the Middle*
CSI: Crime Scene Investigation	*Married … with Children*
Friends	*The Office*
I Dream of Jeannie	*Oprah*
I Love Lucy	*The Practice*
Heroes	*Seinfeld*
Jeopardy	*Six Feet Under*
Jerry Springer	*The Sopranos*
Larry King Live	*Ugly Betty*
Law and Order	*Wheel of Fortune*
Leave It to Beaver	

Treasure Hunt for Puppet Supplies

Players have until the next class/group meeting to bring in any of the following plus whatever their creativity suggests. (Director provides craft/white glue, scissors, and whatever might lend itself to puppet making that is on hand.) Items should *not* be purchased! Empty those drawers and closets!

Broken toys/stuffed animals

Cardboard

Fabric paint

Foam — both hard and soft

Lunch bags

Markers

Miscellaneous ribbons and trim

Needles and thread

Pipe cleaners

Poster paint

Safety pins

Scrap fabric

Socks

Velcro/hook and loop fastener tape

Puppet Choreography Music

"A Wonderful Guy"
"The Addams Family"
"Aquarius"
"All I Want for Christmas"
"All That Jazz"
"Another Opening, Another Show"
"Anything Goes"
"Attack of the Killer Tomatoes"
"Blow, Gabriel, Blow"
"Brush Up Your Shakespeare"
"Camp Granada"
"Do Re Mi"
"Eat It"
"Fish Heads"
"Get a Job"
"Getting to Know You"
"Ghostbusters"
"Go Into Your Dance"
"Grandma Got Run Over by a Reindeer"
"Greased Lightning"
"Happy Talk"
"It's the Hard Knock Life"
"Heaven Hop"
"Hello Dolly"
"Hey, Rickie"
"I Get Around"
"I Love Paris"
"I Saw Mommy Kissing Santa Claus"
"I'd Do Anything"
"Nuttin' for Christmas"
"If You Could See Her"
"June Is Busting Out All Over"
"Kids"
"King Tut"
"Lasagna"
"Leader of the Pack"
"Like a Surgeon"

"Little Deuce Coupe"
"Little Shop of Horrors"
"The Lonely Goatherd"
"Low Rider"
"The Lusty Month of May"
"Matchmaker"
"Monster Mash"
"My Favorite Things"
"There's No Business Like Show Business"
"Peanut Butter"
"Phony Calls"
"You've Got to Pick a Pocket or Two"
"Poisoning Pigeons in the Park"
"The Purple People Eater"
"Put On a Happy Face"
"So Long, Farewell"
"Springtime for Hitler"
"Summer Nights"
"Surfin' Bird"
"The Telephone Hour"
"Youth of the Nation"
"There is Nothing Like a Dame"
"They're Coming to Take Me Away"
"Time Warp"
"Too Darn Hot"
"I'm Gonna Wash That Man Right Outta My Hair"
"We Go Together"
"With a Little Bit O' Luck"
"Yackety Yack"
"Itsy Bitsy Teeny Weeny Yellow Polka Dot Bikini"
"Yoda"
"Dentist!"
"You're the Top"

Resources

Altman, Anna. *Tales Then and Now*. Libraries Unlimited, 2001.

Bara, Renee, and E. Weagele. *The Enneagram Made Easy*. Harper and Row Publishers, 1994.

Barzhof, Hajo and A. Haeblen. *Key Words for Astrology*. York Bead, Marie. Samuel Weisner, Inc., 1996.

Belt, Lynda. *Improv Game Book Two*. Thespis Productions, 1993.

Belt, Lynda, and Rebecca Stockley. *Improvisations Through Theatre Sports*. Thespis Productions, 1995.

Bernardi, Philip. *Improvisation Starters*. F&W Publications, Inc., 1992.

Book, Stephen. *Book on Acting: Improvisation Technique for the Professional Actor in Film, Theatre, and Television*. Silman James Press, 2002.

Brunvand, Jan Harold. *Too Good to be True: A Colossal Book of Urban Legends*. W.W. Norton and Company, Inc., 2001.

————. *Be Afraid, Be Very Afraid: The Book of Scary Urban Legends*. W.W. Norton and Company, Inc., 2004.

————. *The Choking Doberman*. W.W, Norton and Company, Inc., 2003.

————. *Encyclopedia of Urban Legends*. W.W. Norton and Company, Inc., 2002.

————. *The Vanishing Hitchhiker*. W.W, Norton, 1989.

Caltagirone, Dennis. *Theatre Arts: The Dynamics of Acting*. Fourth Edition. NTC Publishing Group, 1997.

Cassady, Marsh. *Acting Games*. Meriwether Publishing Ltd., 1993.

————. *Spontaneous Performance*. Meriwether Publishing Ltd., 2000.

Caruso, Sandra, and Susan Kosoff. *The Young Actor's Book of Improvisation*. Heinemann, 1998.

deVos, Gail. *Storytelling for Young Adults*. Libraries Unlimited, 2001.

————. *Tales, Rumors, and Gossip*. Libraries Unlimited, 1996.

Dockery Young, Richard and Judy. *The Scary Story Reader*. August House Publishers, 1992.

Edelstein, Linda N. *The Writer's Guide to Character Traits*. F&W Publications, Inc., 2004.

Foreman, Kathleen, and Clem Martini. *Something Like a Drug*. Red Deer Press, 1998.

Frager, Robert, ed. *Who Am I?* Penguin Group, 1994.

Hall, William and Paul Killam, eds. *The San Francisco Bay Area Theatresports Playbook, Edition 5.3*. Bay Area TheatreSports, 1998.

Halpern, Charna, Del Close, and Kim Howard Johnson. *Truth in Comedy*. Meriwether Publishing Ltd., 1994.

Halpern, Charna, and Del Close. *Art by Committee*. Meriwether Publishing Ltd., 2006.

Heimburg, Jason and Justin Heimburg. *The Official Movie Plot Generator*. Brothers Heimburg Publishing, LLP., 2004.

Horn, Delton T. *Comedy Improvisation*. Meriwether Publishing Ltd., 1991.

Johnston, Chris. *House of Games*. Taylor & Francis, Inc., 1998.

Johnstone, Keith. *Impro.* Taylor & Francis, Inc., 1987.

———. *Impro for Storytellers.* Taylor & Francis, Inc., 1999.

Keirsey, David. *Please Understand Me II.* Prometheus Nemesis Book Company, Inc., 1998.

Kroger, Otto, and J. Theissen. *Type Talk.* Tilden Press Books, 2002.

Lynn, Bill. *Improvisation for Actors and Writers.* Meriwether Publishing Ltd., 2004.

Neelands, Jonothan, and Tony Goode. *Structuring Drama Work.* Revised Edition. Cambridge University Press, 2000.

Novelly, Maria. *Theatre Games for Young Performers.* Meriwether Publishing Ltd., 1991.

O'Neill, Cecily, et. al. *Drama Guidelines.* Heinemann, 1977.

Peterson, Lenka, and Dan O'Connor. *Kids Take the Stage.* Watson-Guptill Publications, Inc., 1997.

Pollak, Michael. *Musical Improv Comedy.* Masteryear Publishing, 2004.

Salas, Jo. *Improvising Real Life.* Revised Edition. Tusitala, 1993.

Scher, Amy. *101 Ideas for Drama.* Heineman, 1988.

Schmidt, Victoria Lynn. *45 Master Characters.* Writers Digest Books, 2001.

Schnupp, Alvin. *Bravo!* Meriwether Publishing, 2001.

Schwartz, Alvin. *More Scary Stories to Tell in the Dark.* HarperCollins Children's Books, 1986.

———. *Scary Stories 3.* HarperCollins Children's Books, 1991.

———. *Scary Stories to Tell in the Dark.* HarperCollins Children's Books, 1986.

Seham, Amy E. *Whose Improv Is It, Anyway?* University Press of Mississippi, 2001.

Spolin, Viola. *Improvisation for the Theatre.* Third Edition. Northwestern University Press, 1999.

———. *Theatre Games for Rehearsal.* Northwestern University Press, 1985.

———. *Theatre Games for the Classroom.* Northwestern University Press, 1990.

Sternberg, Patricia. *Theatre for Conflict Resolution in the Classroom and Beyond.* Heineman, 1998.

Zimmerman, Suzi. *More Theatre Games for Young Performers.* Meriwether Publishing Ltd., 2004.

Index of Games

About the Authors

Justine Jones
photo by Lee G. Weinland, III

Justine Jones and **Mary Ann Kelley** have collaborated on two drama and theatre curriculum guides for public schools in addition to *Improv Ideas: A Book of Games and Lists* and *Drama Games and Improvs: Games for the Classroom and Beyond* from Meriwether Publishing. They have also collaborated on numerous productions and drama festivals in their former home of Los Alamos, New Mexico.

Justine has taught improvisation and play production on the secondary level for thirty-four years. Her drama education studies have led her to England and Canada as well as several colleges in the U.S. Justine is also trained in psychodrama and drama therapy. Many of the ideas in this book are the result of suggestions from her students. All have been tested and refined in Justine's classrooms for over three decades and have been proven intellectually stimulating and creatively successful.

Justine now resides in London, England, where she continues her work in storytelling and improvisation. She is currently at work on *Mystery and Murder in the Middle School: A guide to writing and producing interactive murder mysteries with secondary school students.* She is furthering her studies at the London Centre for Psychodrama where she is also taking courses in improvisation, playback theatre, and sociodrama. She delights in a massive amount of London theatre.

Mary Ann has taught drama and directed kids in regular school settings and as enrichment for schools and recreation departments for over thirty years. Her recent focus has been the development of plays by and for young people through improvisation. She has directed and taught creative dramatics in multi-grade (grades 3-12) groups for over twenty years. She uses the games in *Improv Ideas* and the lessons in *Drama Games and Improvs* as creative prompts for original student-created plays as well as rehearsal tools for scripted plays. Mary Ann wrote the standards-based drama curriculum for fourth through sixth grades for Los Alamos, NM Public Schools.

Mary Ann Kelley
photo by Lee G. Weinland, III

Mary Ann lives in McIntosh, Florida. She directs children's plays — both scripted and kid-created; directs and techs with adults; attends as many theatrical events as possible; and voraciously reads everything from plays and classics to "trashy crime fiction." She is now at work on *Creating Theatre in Twenty Hours*, a step-by-step guide designed for recreation leaders and teachers with too little time. *Creating Theatre in Twenty Hours* is a compilation of the techniques she used in fifteen years of teaching two-week summer school sessions in creative dramatics, each culminating in performances of original plays.

Order Form

Meriwether Publishing Ltd.
PO Box 7710
Colorado Springs CO 80933-7710
Phone: 800-937-5297   Fax: 719-594-9916
Website: www.meriwether.com

Please send me the following books:

_____ **Drama Games and Improvs #BK-B296**   **$22.95**
by Justine Jones and Mary Ann Kelley
Games for the classroom and beyond

_____ **Improv Ideas #BK-B283**   **$22.95**
by Justine Jones and Mary Ann Kelley
A book of games and lists

_____ **112 Acting Games #BK-B277**   **$17.95**
by Gavin Levy
A comprehensive workbook of theatre games

_____ **Drama Games and Acting Exercises #BK-B311**   **$17.95**
by Rod Martin
177 games and activities

_____ **Theatre Games for Young Performers #BK-B188** **$17.95**
by Maria C. Novelly
Improvisations and exercises for developing acting skills

_____ **Group Improvisation #BK-B259**   **$16.95**
by Peter Gwinn with additional material by Charna Halpern
The manual of ensemble improv games

_____ **Acting Games for Individual Performers**   **$17.95**
#BK-297
by Gavin Levy
A comprehensive workbook of 110 acting exercises

These and other fine Meriwether Publishing books are available at your local bookstore or direct from the publisher. Prices subject to change without notice. Check our website or call for current prices.

Name: _____ e-mail: _____

Organization name: _____

Address: _____

City: _____ State: _____

Zip: _____ Phone: _____

❏ **Check enclosed**
❏ **Visa / MasterCard / Discover / Am. Express#** _____

Signature: _____   *Expiration date:* _____
                      (required for credit card orders)

Colorado residents: Please add 3% sales tax.
Shipping: Include $3.95 for the first book and 75¢ for each additional book ordered.

❏ *Please send me a copy of your complete catalog of books and plays.*